What Christian Leaders Have Said About

LOOKING UP THE AISLE?

Few people have the commitment to biblical marriage coupled with the experience and creative insight of Dave and Joyce Ames. *Looking Up the Aisle?* breaks new ground and is trans-cultural. I expect to use it in marriage counselling as well as marriage preparation. A must on every Christian counsellor's bookshelf.

Dr Raju Abraham, MBBS, MRCP (UK), MRCP (Ire)
Chairman of the Association of Biblical Counsellors

The realistic approach of *Looking Up the Aisle?* will, I am sure, give a very strong foundation to many marriages.

David Alton MP

Congratulations on a concise, clear and well-structured workbook. *Looking Up the Aisle?* covers a lot of ground in a short time without making any omissions or assumptions that would be unhelpful.

Andy Butcher
Former Editor, *Christian Family* magazine

How grateful we must be for those like Dave and Joyce Ames who share their insights and sensitivity into human relationships. *Looking Up the Aisle?* is perceptive, full of practical advice and soundly based in Scripture. It deserves the widest possible use.

General Eva Burrows
International Commander, Salvation Army

I am encouraged at the initiative that *Mission to Marriage* is taking. Clearly this is one of the key issues of our day. The material produced is designed to create a thoughtful response from couples preparing for marriage. I warmly commend it as a constructive contribution to the work of the church in Britain today.

Clive Calver
Director, Evangelical Alliance

Not only is *Looking Up the Aisle?* excellent for those for whom it is primarily intended, but it would be challenging and enlightening for couples married for some years.

Colonel Sidney Gauntlett
Salvation Army, Marriage Enrichment

We found it fascinating to discover the kind of ground that you cover, and learned from your insights.

David and Joyce Huggett
Marriage Fulfilment Seminars

Looking Up the Aisle? is full of realistic, down-to-earth good sense, laced with humour and packed with practical examples. Thoroughly biblical, this book tackles real life issues in a positive and manageable way.

David Jackman
Minister of Above Bar Church, Southampton

The family is the cornerstone of society, and marriage is the foundation of the family. We neglect preparation for this relationship at great peril. *Looking Up the Aisle?* takes biblical, practical and challenging steps towards reversing the trend of marriage breakdown caused by poor preparation.

Dr Michael Schluter
Director of Family Base

Looking Up the Aisle? is very stimulating, full of insight, and raises many vital issues. The emphasis on character rather than technique, running throughout the book, is excellent.

Terry Virgo
Leader of New Frontiers International

Looking Up the Aisle?

A Couple's Guide to Friendship, Romance and Marriage

DAVE AND JOYCE AMES

KINGSWAY PUBLICATIONS
EASTBOURNE

First published 1989
Second edition 1991

Front cover design by Taffy Davies

British Library Cataloguing in Publication Data

Ames, Dave
Looking up the aisle.
1. Marriage—Christian viewpoints
I. Title II. Ames, Joyce
261.8'3581

ISBN 0-86065-943-7

Printed in Great Britain for
KINGSWAY PUBLICATIONS LTD
1 St Anne's Road, Eastbourne, E Sussex BN21 3UN by
Richard Clay Ltd, Bungay, Suffolk
Typeset by Nuprint Ltd, Harpenden, Herts.

This book is dedicated to:

Brian and Elaine Abshire

Ted and Ann Bleymaier

Steve and Helen Clark

Dave and Carita Lindemann

Vern and Libby Gauthier

John and Gina Pearson

Joe and Cathy Stanley

David and Cheryl Zumwalt

All were once a part of our singles ministry and elected to conduct their courtship according to the principles laid out in this book. Without exception they have commented on how much they appreciated having that foundation for their courtship which in turn provided an effective launching-pad for their marriage.

Acknowledgements

We must acknowledge a debt to *Before You Say 'I Do'* by Wes Roberts and H Norman Wright (Harvest House, USA). If it were not for using it in the days of our singles ministry, we very likely would not have even thought of a workbook for engaged couples.

We are grateful that Roger Chouler was sufficiently impressed with the concept and content to donate his services as an illustrator.

We also want to thank Care for The Family, David and Joyce Huggett, Hazel Barclay and Colonel Sidney Gauntlett of the Salvation Army, for their in-depth scrutiny of this material prior to publication. This was accomplished in a real spirit of Christian unity, that an effective tool might be available for use in the broadest possible segment of those holding the Scriptures in high regard.

We would like to thank Mary-Jo Taylor for permission to quote her poem *For You Were Truly a Man*.

We are also indebted to all those who took the time to review the material in order to give it their personal endorsement: Dr Raju Abraham, David Alton, Andy Butcher, General Eva Burrows, Clive Calver, David Jackman, Dr Michael Schluter and Terry Virgo.

Contents

Introduction

It has been said that a great deal more preparation goes into obtaining a driving licence than a marriage licence.

Christian and secular marriage counsellors both agree that communication problems are a major factor in the breakdown of relationships. Christians would go on to identify a more basic level of problem potential: human selfishness. It is at this point that Christian and secular marriage and premarriage teaching part company because secular society has no moral or ethical framework for dealing with matters of character, and selfishness is a matter of character.

The *roots* of marriage breakdown are not found in poor communication or the lack of skill in working through conflicts. These are necessary skills, but they are technical in nature. Successful marriage is not simply a technical matter—it is a matter of character.

God's goal for the individual believer is to be conformed to the image of his Son. Jesus Christ did not die just that we might have a home in heaven some day. He died that we might have a relationship with the Father, and the goal of that relationship with the Father is to develop the character of his Son. Salvation is not a destination—it is a journey. Christian marriage is intended to be two people on the same journey.

Couples equipped with the character of Christ have an ability to weather the storms of life that technical relationship skills alone cannot provide. Communication skills are valuable tools. It is character which determines the sensitivity with which we use these tools and, in some instances, whether we use them at all or just allow the relationship to deteriorate.

This workbook will have a heavy emphasis on communication because we see communication as the life-blood of a relationship. Just as the bloodstream is the body's delivery system so communication is the main vehicle supplying the relationship. Couples using this workbook will spend a fair amount of time communicating practical issues in private sessions, blending their positions on the biblical concepts we are presenting. Hopefully, someone overseeing the study will elaborate on the issues.

Warning

This is not a 'one-stop' marriage qualification. No one book can provide all of the desirable printed resources. The objective of this particular book is not so much to supply information as to facilitate communication. Each chapter contains a narrative followed by a few questions to be answered separately by each partner. These answers then form a basis for meaningful dialogue on various facets of marriage. The narratives are not meant to give exhaustive coverage of the topic, but we do believe that they will provide a sufficient framework of understanding to help couples develop sound, reasonable expectations, objectives and priorities. We have included a suggested reading list at the end of every chapter to expand understanding in each area. This reading list directs the reader to specific chapters in various books, to keep the focus on one topic at a time.

The purposes of this publication are to help couples:

Develop some basic principles of courtship which will assure maximum communication and blending.

Gain a full, biblical understanding of love. Love is the most ill-defined word in the English language, but the Scriptures resolve the 'mystery'.

Define marriage in God's terms.

Develop a biblical concept of self in marriage by discussing some basic needs and how we should expect them to be met.

Understand the importance of communication as the vehicle of their relationship. And learn some of the skills and pitfalls of communication.

Clarify role expectations. The Bible cuts a straight line between male chauvinism and women's lib.

Adjust expectations. Many people enter into marriage with unrealistic and unscriptural expectations.

Blend the result of differing backgrounds and temperaments.

Gain the necessary equipment to resolve conflicts effectively. People who agree on everything seldom marry each other. It almost seems to be God's plan. Consequently it helps to be prepared to resolve differences.

Understand the need to give and receive forgiveness in order to walk in the freedom of a clear conscience.

Understand the biblical philosophy of finances.

Understand the new role of parents as in-laws.

Develop a full biblical understanding of sex. The Bible introduces sexual love as the celebration of the most intimate of all relationships, whereas contemporary thinking often sees it as the motive for relationships.

Too many couples are entering into marriage with what can best be described as an incomplete knowledge of what it really means to be totally committed to another human being. This is not limited to secular marriages. Secular philosophy has had a much greater influence in shaping the thoughts of Christians than we sometimes recognise. This influence leaves many believers with a distorted understanding of a Christian world-view. They are then incapable of responding from a Christian perspective in certain situations.

As we read Matthew 22:36–40 there can be no doubt that Christian maturity is measured against a plumb-line of love. The way we function in relationships is a fairly accurate barometer of our spiritual growth. This, coupled with the knowledge that marriage is our priority human relationship, gives special urgency to properly equipping couples for this pivotal human relationship.

This workbook is an attempt to give insights into very practical ways of earthing our faith into the everyday living out of the marriage commitment.

'What is your pleasure?'

MATURITY IS:

Conducting my life in the understanding that success is a by-product of service.

Matthew 23:11: 'The greatest among you will be your servant.'

I

Some Basic Courtship Considerations

Clearly the relationships in which we are involved vary considerably. They vary in characteristics and in the amount of responsibility they require. Close and intimate friendships are characterised by commitment and vulnerability. We are committed and open to each other in a way which brings us under the influence of the other's ethics and direction in life.

Checking the Foundation

One thing is clear, the major requirement for deepening a friendship should be the possession of the same basic goals for our lives. Christians, especially, should be cautious about allowing themselves to be influenced by people who do not have the same life goals. Christian life goals are a matter of character. We cannot allow pagan concepts to influence our character development. This does not mean that we cannot be friends with an unbeliever—obviously, we cannot reach people for Christ if we insulate ourselves from non-Christian company. It is the level of friendship that we must be realistic about. We cannot have a deep friendship without allowing that friendship to influence us, because that is the very nature of a deep friendship. In making ourselves vulnerable to each other, we are saying, 'I trust you to influence me'.

Marriage is more than romance. It is a commitment to friendship, the most intimate friendship. Before we enter into such a relationship we should first of all be convinced that there is a proper basis for it. So not only must we establish that we have mutual life goals, but we need reasonable assurance that each partner has adequate commitment to those goals to persevere. This will, in the long run, determine the value of the relationship. On a somewhat lesser scale is the need to discover if there is sufficient common interest and taste to enjoy living together. These, plus a host of varying expectations, require vast amounts of communication.

Although the decision to enter a 'courtship' is based on sufficient common interest (we are using this term to include values and tastes), the purpose of courtship is to explore, ensure and *expand* that base of common interest.

Relationships can be Expensive

There is no relationship without cost. The price is paid in areas of disagreement and divergence. The fact that we must spend time in activities or surroundings which we find distasteful in support of a relationship is the cost of that relationship. We count the cost when we are deprived of activities and things we enjoy. If one marriage partner loves camping out and the other hates it, a price must be paid either by one enduring or the other being deprived.

The cost of a relationship can never be totally abolished, but it can be minimised by extending the common interests. We can blend our ideas and tastes. Through patient, considerate dialogue on an area of disagreement partners frequently discover common threads to build upon. For example, a man who loves camping generally loves the outdoors. It may be that his partner also loves the outdoors but feels a need to limit it to small doses. That love of the outdoors is one strand of common interest.

The next question is, could they enjoy the great outdoors without actually camping? It would be helpful for him to give an expanded definition of camping, while his partner listens carefully. Through asking questions she may find that the really objectionable facets of camping can be avoided through proper equipment and procedure. Even if camping is still a complete turn-off for her there are plenty of creative ways to enjoy the outdoors without camping.

There are literally dozens of issues which are best explored prior to marriage. Most will be of greater magnitude than camping. But even an issue such as camping can become rather central if it is of importance to one partner. Exploration for the purpose of understanding and negotiation is the actual relationship-building process. The more significant areas, such as goals and values, naturally have the highest priority, but fears, desires, sport and hobbies are just as rich in their potential to develop a relationship. By the way, we don't recommend a camping honeymoon—we've heard of a few that have been disasters!

Value over Cost

Marriage partners should be best friends. Valuable friendships are not found, they are built. In one sense it is simply a matter of keeping the value far ahead of the cost.

We give value to a relationship through selflessly ministering to each other's needs, and we reduce the cost by blending tastes and interests. This selfless attitude is mainly a matter of character, while pooling our interests is mainly technique. Both are necessary. We also need some technique to earth Christian character into the situation at hand. Without some amount of what can be called 'relationship skill' we will commit many 'well-meaning blunders' which can cause a lot of hurt.

Conversely, all of the technique or relationship skill in the world is useless in and of itself. It is the character behind the skill which assures both sound motivation and genuineness. In our marriage counselling we have met many who have a good understanding of how they should be treating their partner, but they lack the proper motivation. Still others go through the motions but without any real desire to improve the relationship.

Character as a Criterion

Character is the motivation behind right actions:

Responsibility is a desirable character attribute. Can a person be counted on to do what they agree to do? If they fail will they assume responsibility for the failure or blame someone else?

Honesty is a character quality demonstrated in the way we deal with expense accounts, time cards and the extra money accidentally given us in change.

Respect for others, or the lack of it, is easily demonstrated through our level of consideration. There is no reason to suppose we will be any better, in the long run, at demonstrating respect towards our partner than we are to our parents and relatives.

Self-discipline could be considered the 'main bearing' in our character. It is the quality which determines whether we will have the diligence to develop the rest of our character.

All of the foregoing principles apply to any relationship, but we are not talking about just any relationship. We are discussing a relationship between two people considering Christian marriage which brings an added physical dimension. More than spirit and soul we also have a body. (Maybe you have already noticed!)

The sexual drives and attractiveness of this body are a part of the magnetism which draws male and female together and makes possible the celebration of that relationship. This is not only normal, it is healthy and should typify any marriage or engagement regardless of age. Later we will consider exploring this dimension to the full potential God created it to have.

Complicating Factor

However, at this point, sex is also a complicating factor. Sexual intercourse is the celebration of a relationship, not the reason for it. And as you are well aware, the Bible limits this celebration to marriage. The first complication is the fact that we have such a strong compulsion to celebrate the relationship before it is completely established. The second is the fact that we tend to make ourselves miserable by exploring the limits to which we can resist the temptation to go all the way.

Dating practices that have grown up as our 'permissive society' has developed will not stand the test of scriptural reasoning or even common sense. There are several very sound reasons for couples, laying a foundation for marriage, to keep physical expressions of their love to a minimum.

Even a kiss can be like the sharp end of a wedge which has the power to pierce our body chemistry, split open our emotional equilibrium and lead desires towards the bedroom far too prematurely.

Speaking from a psychological perspective, we understand why this wedge seems to throw the door of desire wider open with every new pleasure. It is because pleasure-seeking is a bottomless pit, never satisfied. Jeremiah 17:9 tells us 'The heart is deceitful.' It certainly plays tricks on us. It tells us that if we could just advance the intimacy of our relationship to the next step we would be satisfied to hold at that level until the wedding. But it does not work that way. We are not satisfied. We may not actually continue escalating the physical side of our relationship, but each level of intimacy brings a more intense motivation to advance.

Spiritually we understand the true nature of sex is giving rather than getting, therefore it is dishonest to raise expectations in our partner that we cannot rightfully fulfil. And all the more so if our motive is to seek our own pleasure. A young man once told us, following a talk on sex and relationships, that the reason he fondled his fiancée's breasts was for her pleasure and not his. Even if this were true, he is still guilty of bringing her to a state of desire that he cannot rightfully satisfy. Is it love which drives one human to reduce another to a state of highly charged expectation and desire when no more can be done, or is it lust?

Hands-Off Courtship?

We are aware that the idea that couples go through a courtship with little or no caressing seems out of touch with reality. By this point in the relationship almost any kiss, with the possible exception of a peck on the cheek, becomes a transmitter of sexual messages. A lot of couples involved with our singles ministry have taken the challenge of 'hands-off' courting and have since thanked us for it, even though at the time they wondered if they could not get by with something a bit less conservative.

We have not discussed what may well be the most far-reaching effect of the physical side of our courtship. To bring this into line, let us review some of the factors mentioned earlier.

There is both value and cost to a relationship. The value is enhanced as the character of Christ is produced in our lives and practised in our relationship.

The cost is reduced through blending of tastes and interests. Communication is the key to blending. Consider the effect that these factors have on each other:

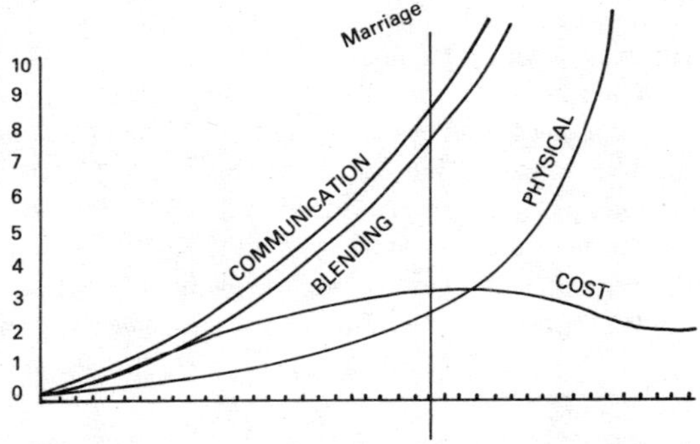

The first chart is an ideal courtship, Physical intimacy and cost are low, while communication and blending are high.

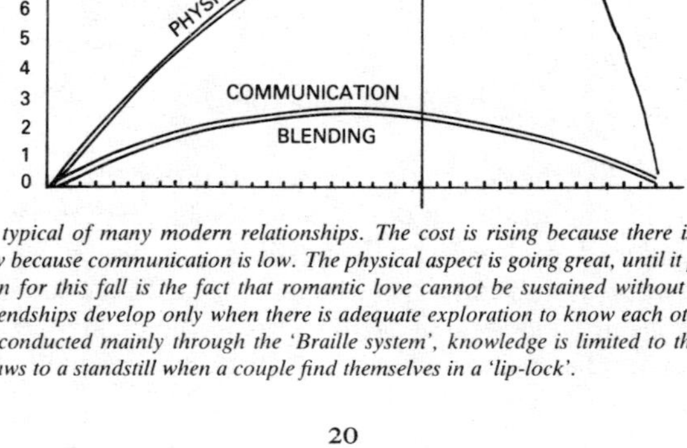

The second is typical of many modern relationships. The cost is rising because there is no blending. Blending is low because communication is low. The physical aspect is going great, until it peaks and falls off. The reason for this fall is the fact that romantic love cannot be sustained without an underlying friendship. Friendships develop only when there is adequate exploration to know each other. When this exploration is conducted mainly through the 'Braille system', knowledge is limited to the body. Communication draws to a standstill when a couple find themselves in a 'lip-lock'.

Physical intimacy promises to seal and secure the relationship, but this is a deception. Relationships become secure only when we know our partner and we are known by them. This is the objective of courtship. We can trust God that all of the other equipment will function as advertised.

We may have some desire to be appreciated for our physical appearance, but most of us would hope to be desired for what we are down inside. The thought that our body is our greatest asset is a very precarious basis for a relationship. Even if disease or injury does not nullify our appearance, the law of gravity will soon alter it significantly!

The following questions should be answered by each partner separately, then answers should be compared and discussed.

1 Romans 8:29 tells us that God's goal in our relationship with him is to conform us to the image of his Son. This means that he intends us to develop the character of Christ. As an honest evaluation, on a scale of 1 to 10. How committed are you to this same goal?

. . . .

2 What are you presently doing to reach this goal?

. . . .

. . . .

3 For the purpose of this question, temporarily forget that marriage is your intention. Something totally unforeseen could occur to preclude it. Consider this as simply a very close and enjoyable relationship in order to answer the following question. How will this relationship contribute to both of you reaching towards the goal of Romans 8:29?

. . . .

. . . .

4 What limits on physical intimacy do you consider appropriate in this relationship?

a Occasional hugs and short periods of hand holding ☐
b Plus short 'good-night' kisses ☐
c Plus long lingering 'good-night' kisses ☐
d Nice cuddly periods of kisses and hugs on the sofa ☐
e Plus a little bit of petting ☐
f Petting including anything short of 'going all the way'. ☐

A syndicated advice column in the United States carried the following:

Dear Ann Landers,

When I was twenty I married a man I was madly in love with. (Or so I thought.) After eighteen years of pain I have decided to leave. I now realise I looked for the wrong things.

These are the questions a woman should ask herself before she marries:

(1) Does he have mature and realistic goals?
(2) Does he treat me with respect and consideration?
(3) Is he reliable and honest?
(4) Does he like children?
(5) Does he get along with his family and friends?
(6) Is he responsible about money?
(7) Will he be interested in growth and self-improvement?
(8) If a sense of humour is important to you, does he have one?

If I had asked myself these questions before I rushed into marriage, I would have been a lot better off.

I hope you will print my letter for the benefit of the young women who think they are in love and are willing to overlook 'a few things' because they are afraid that they can't live without the guy.

This is sound judgement but nothing beyond the reach of average mortals. We personally think that many who make poor choices are aware of such commonsense criteria but choose to ignore it.

5 Which of the following notions would you say was the most frequent reason why intelligent people fail to ask such questions?

a Marriage means freedom from parental authority ☐
b The prospective partner has money ☐
c Anything is better than singleness ☐
d There is no one else who would be willing to marry them ☐
e Their 'shelf life' as an eligible marriage partner is about to expire ☐
f They are on the rebound from a broken relationship ☐
g Other ☐

Further reading

Dave and Joyce Ames, *Second Honeymoon*, (Kingsway), Chapter 1.
Ed Wheat, *Love Life for Every Married Couple*, (Marshalls), Chapter 9.
John and Janet Houghton, *A Touch of Love*, (Kingsway), Chapter 2.
Ian and Ruth Coffey, *Marriage—the Early Years*, (Kingsway), Chapter 1.

MATURITY IS:

The understanding that if love is not viewed more as a commitment to be entered into than a desire to be fulfilled, neither will happen.

1 Corinthians 13:4–7: 'Love is patient, love is kind. It does not envy, it does not boast, it is not proud. It is not rude, it is not self-seeking, it is not easily angered, it keeps no record of wrongs. Love does not delight in evil but rejoices with the truth. It always protects, always trusts, always hopes, always perseveres.'

2

Love Is

MATURITY IS:

Recognising that real love is much more an action than an emotion.
1 John 3:17–18: 'If anyone has material possessions and sees his brother in need but has no pity on him, how can the love of God be in him? Dear children, let us not love with words or tongue but with actions and in truth.'

'I love you, I can't live without you.'
'Every bone in my body aches for you.'
'I want to spend the rest of my days with you.'
'You are the only one who could possibly make me happy.'

These are very flattering remarks and there would be no reason to doubt their sincerity. There is nothing really wrong with them, but then there is not quite enough right about them either. They simply tell us that someone has some very specific desires, aches and pains. One thing that must be pointed out is the fact that these remarks, however romantic-sounding, are all self-centred. The speaker is concerned with his life, his feelings and his happiness. **Saying 'I love you' is only a declaration of taste. 'I will love you' is a commitment. The first has little meaning without the second. Romance can be selfish.**

English is an effective language but it has its shortcomings. The word 'love' is one of them. It covers such a wide variety of conditions that it is less specific than a weather forecast. Greek, on the other hand, has numerous words that we translate as love. There is nothing authoritative about Greek, but there is about the New Testament which was written in Greek. By understanding the way the Greeks separated various facets of love we have a much better idea of where God places his emphasis.

Three Greek terms that are particularly involved in marriage are *eros, phileo* and *agape*.

Each of these expressions of love should be part of every marriage. Eros love is typified by its appeal to the physical senses, therefore is closely associated with sex. Not every physical attraction is sexual and there is more to eros than sex. Eros is also the mysterious 'force' on which songwriters seem to concentrate.

Eros love is the chemistry that causes us to want to make physical contact—it is the butterflies in the tummy, the excitement that rises when we see or hear that special one and we want to say 'you flip my switches', or 'you float my boat'. It is shown not only in the 'act of marriage', but in the giving of affection throughout the day. There is no need that 'hello/goodbye' kisses, an arm around the shoulder, a good cuddle should diminish with the years. It will continue all through marriage as long as it has a good foundation of friendship.

Phileo love is a friendship love based on common interest. It is not a physical attraction but a psychological affinity. Marriage partners should be best friends and as such should be able to share their thoughts and feelings, interests and values, tastes and aspirations. We tend to 'like' those people who are 'like' us. Common interests are not the only attraction. We may also admire people who have skills and strengths which complement our weaknesses. This admiration can also contribute to our basis for phileo love.

One of the greatest distinctives of phileo love is team work. C S Lewis says, 'Lovers are always talking to each other about their love; friends hardly ever talk about their friendship. Lovers are normally face to face, absorbed in each other; friends are side by side, absorbed in some common interest.'[1]

Phileo is a much more level-headed relationship than eros, much more stable and therefore much safer. Eros love can be likened to an affair with a box of chocolates. You can love them so much that you eat them all up, then there is no more affair. Sophocles wrote of the god Eros as 'the god which forgot all reason'. Eros without the underpinning of phileo is an open door to a self-indulgent, self-destructing relationship.

Eros love is the capacity to celebrate a relationship. It could be said that phileo is the relationship. It is the day-in day-out caring which

[1] C S Lewis, *The Four Loves* (Fontana, 1981), p 58.

enables us to celebrate. It is easy to care for a friend, but what happens when our 'friend' is not acting friendly?

Agape love makes no requirement on the object of its love. It is neither a physical nor a psychological attraction. It does not love 'because of'. Often it loves 'in spite of'. It is a matter of the will. Agape is much more a decision and an investment than an emotion or a feeling. Agape is investing my resources in another person's well-being. The profit from the investment goes to the one being loved and then only indirectly to the lover.

Agape love is also the mark of a Christian. John 13:35 says, 'All men will know that you are my disciples if you love one another.' We can see the reason if we go to the opposite end of the scale and focus on selfishness. It is a dividing issue between Christian and secular thinking.

Secular humanism says that anyone who thinks he can be anything but selfish is deceiving himself. Consequently secular logic views selfishness within oneself as a force to be harnessed and in others as a weakness to be exploited. It is a fact of life and a right to be defended. They do, on occasion, have pangs of conscience regarding self-centredness. But secular society has nothing upon which to build such a philosophy. Selfishness is a part of basic survival instinct, therefore it is impossible to avoid being concerned with self when one does not believe anyone else is. The world's motto is, 'You have got to look out for yourself because no one else will.'

It is only the knowledge of a Sovereign Lord, interested in our well-being, that allows anyone to develop a logical stand against selfishness. Aside from the revelation of God there is no data which would encourage or allow any thinking person to develop a truly unselfish philosophy of life.

Not only do Christians have the necessary basis for such a concept, but we know that we are commanded to live out a standard unselfishness, far surpassing a mere social grace.

It is easy to lose sight of this in a society which has actually institutionalised the demanding of its rights. Christian teaching reverses this trend by focusing on personal responsibility.

' "Teacher, which is the greatest commandment in the Law?" Jesus replied: "Love the Lord your God with all your heart and with all your soul and with all your mind. This is the first and greatest commandment. And the second is like it: Love your neighbour as yourself. All the Law and the Prophets hang on these two commandments" ' (Matthew 22:36–40).

This is one of the most significant texts in the Bible. The Lord Jesus Christ is saying that all of the Scripture is summed up as a love relationship with God and a love relationship with our neighbour. This would mean that all of the degrees in theology, faithful church attendance and good works are worthless if we do not have it together in this one area. **Love is the plumb-line against which all spiritual maturity is measured.**

The fact that we are commanded to love even our enemies tells us that love is more of a decision than a feeling. It is more than a decision to buy flowers for your lover or plan a romantic dinner. It is a continuous attitude which influences much more mundane, everyday decisions. It is an act of love to roll the toothpaste tube if we know that squeezing it in the middle irritates our partner. Little considerations such as replacing a magazine in the rack rather than leaving it lying on the couch, bringing the milk in off the step or refilling the ice cube tray, and a thousand little tailor-made considerations. 1 Corinthians 13:4–8a gives a definition of love that sounds like a description of consideration and integrity personified.

> **Love is patient** *about dirty clothes left strewn around the bedroom,*
> **love is kind** *enough not to leave them there in the first place.*
> **It does not envy** *her husband taking clients out to lunch,*
> **it does not boast** *about the wonderful lunch he had at company expense,*
> **it is not proud** *that she has more Bible knowledge than he does.*
> **It is not rude** *in pointing out that she sometimes fails to apply it,*
> **it is not self-seeking** *considers family over self-fulfilment,*
> **it is not easily angered** *over mud on the floor,*
> **it keeps no record of wrongs** *or times she has told him to wipe his feet.*
> **Love does not delight in evil** *he actually feels bad about forgetting,*
> **but rejoices with the truth** *he is thrilled when he finally does remember.*
> **It always protects** *he even puts the toilet seat down,*
> **always trusts** *she believes the best about him,*
> **always hopes** *and actually believes some day she will have him trained,*
> **always perseveres** *in spite of discouraging setbacks.*
> **Love never fails** *when continually applied.*

There is obviously a quality about agape love that brings out our total positive resources, making them available to the one being loved. It is this quality that makes it a commitment type of love which is discerning but not discriminating or demanding.

It is, however, more than a commitment of our best efforts—it is a commitment to what is best for the object of that love. This means it is committed to doing exactly the right thing. Doing the best or the right thing is central to the definition of agape love, because it allows us to see that love is not some sugar-plum notion—it is an investment in the future as well.

'There are times when we may not find each other attractive.'

A mother does not spank a child to get even with it. It is to help the child develop sufficient self-discipline to save it future heartache. By the same token love is called upon to find a constructive way to point out a selfish behaviour in my partner. It is not love when the concern is the fact that I am being inconvenienced, but it is when the concern is for the damage that is being done to my partner and our relationship.

Dr Ed Wheat in his book *Love Life for Every Married Couple*[1] makes some very sage comments regarding the nature of love:

> What you think about love will control your behaviour.
>
> When reason is excluded from love's excitements what results is not love at all but lust, infatuation, or empty sentimentality.
>
> If you do what comes naturally you will be wrong almost every time. Love is an art to be learned and a discipline to be maintained.

[1] Ed Wheat, *Love Life for Every Married Couple* (Marshalls, 1984) pp 50, 51 and 54.

Real love is always a choice backed up by action.

Love is always doing the very best for the object of one's love . . . and there is nothing mysterious about that.

All of this makes love sound a bit of a drudgery, hard work and not very romantic. Agape does not detract from romance—it insures the quality. It is the only thing that can guarantee that romance will endure.

Phileo love would do quite nicely but unfortunately phileo cannot always be counted on. There are times when we do not find each other attractive and even feel like we are not in love. We may have a head filled with reasons why we do not. This is when agape love takes over and with our will we continue to show forth acts of love, doing what is best for our partner whether they deserve or respond to it or not. This type of loving commitment can bring a marriage through the rough times and into full blossom again.

Love is the antithesis of selfishness, it consists of investing one's own resources in the well-being of another.

Some Practical Steps

1 As marriage partners view themselves with regard to the prospect of being loved there is something to be said for considering the phileo model. That is this, should I rely on the agape love of my partner or should I strive to be the type of person that my partner could easily love even if no agape love were available?

. . . .

. . . .

. . . .

Please explain your answer.

. . . .

. . . .

. . . .

2 List at least five things that you could do to be a bargain for your partner. What are some things you could do or habits you could develop which would make your partner feel glad he or she has a relationship with you?

. . . .

. . . .

. . . .

. . . .

. . . .

3 After you have discussed your answers with your partner discuss what you perceive to be God's intended purpose for each of the three types of love, how they support and complement each other.

. . . .

. . . .

. . . .

4 What do you see as the primary cause of marriage breakdown?

. . . .

. . . .

5 What specific areas of marriage will cause the most conflict with your own selfishness?

. . . .

. . . .

. . . .

6 What do you think would be the main secret of maintaining a healthy sex life into one's seventies and even beyond?

. . . .

. . . .

. . . .

7 Modelling is a very important part of learning, therefore we learn a lot from our parents about life, love and marriage. The example they modelled before us can have a strong effect, either positive or negative. Our parents may not have been Christian, or even if they were they could have been the victims of some erroneous ideas or traditions. Most of us have to admit that although our parents may not have had an ideal marriage, we have learned a lot of valuable lessons from them. In the event you lack this parental model, perhaps you could use another marriage relationship which influenced you—a relative or close family relationship.

How do you rate your parents' (or substitute model) marriage on a scale of 1 to 10 in the following areas (10 being the highest):

a Romance, it was no secret that they were very much in love ☐

b Friendship, they seemed to share a lot of common interests and projects together ☐

c Commitment, there was no doubt that they were willing to sacrifice for each other ☐

d We were a very physically demonstrative family, plenty of kisses and hugs all round ☐

8 List at least five practical things your parents did to demonstrate love to each other. The father earning a living or the mother keeping house could rightly be listed but try listing much more specific, yet practical, expressions of love.

....

....

....

....

....

9 List at least five things you observed from your parents regarding love that will be a help in your marriage. These could be the positive side of your parents' shortcomings, eg a young man may have noticed that his father never took his mother into consideration when purchasing the family car. Consequently he could see making car-purchasing a joint effort as an expression of love.

....

....

....

....

....

Further reading
Dave and Joyce Ames, *Second Honeymoon* (Kingsway), Chapter 2.
Ed Wheat, *Love Life for Every Married Couple* (Marshalls), Chapters 5 and 10.

MATURITY IS:

Conducting my life in the understanding that success is a by-product of service.

Matthew 23:11: 'The greatest among you will be your servant.'

3

A Synergystic Effect

'Between us we have the tools to do the job.'

We are all created in God's image, but because of the Fall that image is twisted. That twist is not limited to lumbering us with a sinful nature. Our physical bodies and even our mental capabilities are less than those provided for Adam and Eve before the Fall.

The fact that human beings have quite a variation of abilities and shortcomings attests to the fact that we are not all twisted in the same areas. Some people are very mathematically inclined, others excel in verbal skills. Some people are very spatially oriented which makes them good with their hands, but even that varies all the way from house building to brain surgery. Some people are very sensitive to colour and design, others to tone and movement, which may manifest itself in art, athletics or music. Some people seem to have a natural knack for making money, while others have a marvellous ability for getting along without it.

There are also personality characteristics which are manifested both as strengths and weaknesses. People with analytical minds have a great tendency to be negative. The outgoing are frequently undisciplined and possibly obnoxious. The decisive person can be impetuous. The self-confident leader can be insensitive and inconsiderate.

We must have things in common as a basis for a relationship. The common ground is most generally in significant areas such as common goals, ethics and interests. It is not hard to imagine a relationship where the common interests dictated a certain amount of duplication of skills and abilities. It is not too hard to picture this when one considers interests such as tennis, oil painting or bike riding. But the handful of abilities involved in our areas of common interest are like a postage stamp on a bed sheet compared to all that goes into making us the unique individuals we are.

However, God is sovereign and he knows our strengths and our weaknesses. He knows where we need help as well as where we have a special ability to help others. He constantly brings others into our lives who are able to bring out the best that we have, as well as those traits of which we are most ashamed; the one for his glory and the other for correction. This is part of God's character development curriculum. He is committed to developing the character of Christ in our lives, most of which is accomplished through our interaction with other people.

Have you ever noticed how God has a tendency to match up the strong, overbearing with the meek and shy, the perfectionist with the reckless, the lazy with the energetic, the silly with the sober? It is not simply a case of blessed are the meek for they shall inherit the overbearing. God has a goal in mind. He is not as interested in comfortable relationships as with developing the character of Christ in our lives.

There is another dimension which we like to call a *synergistic effect*. It is obviously an obscure word, but we think it will help to develop a handhold on a specific truth. A synergistic effect is defined as two substances coming together to create a greater effect than the sum of the two could achieve separately. For instance, some drugs cannot be taken together for this reason. When drugs which cause drowsiness are prescribed we are frequently advised to avoid all alcohol intake because this particular quality is heightened by the synergistic effect with the alcohol. God certainly does this with marriage partners. He brings two people together with the right balance of gifts and abilities and sufficient tension in their tastes, ideas and opinions to draw the best out of each other. Consequently the two working together will be much more effective than the combined total of their efforts if the two had stayed separate.

Some Practical Steps

Use a pencil for this exercise. In column 1 list your partner's character, temperament or personality strengths. List yours next to your partner's in column 2. In column 3 list your partner's skills and abilities. In column 4 list your skills and abilities.

Column 1 Your fiancée's strengths of temperament, character or personality	**Column 2** Your strengths of temperament, character or personality
....	....
....	....
....	....
....	....
....	....
....	....
....	....
....	....
....	....
....	....

Column 3 Your fiancée's skills and abilities	Column 4 Your skills and abilities
....	....
....	....
....	....
....	....
....	....
....	....
....	....
....	....
....	....

Compare your lists. From your partner's lists, add additional qualities and strengths you may have overlooked. You will undoubtedly observe several areas where one has strengths and the other seems to have weaknesses. Please do not consider this as a score-board of who is bringing the most into the marriage. There are two reasons for this: first, there is no way to place a value on any one quality, and second, a quality considered to be a weakness is frequently only a counterbalance to assure that a strength is not misused.

It has been said that a negative character quality is a positive quality misused. For instance it may be that, viewed at this point, the woman has a quality of cautious practicality and by comparison the man seems a reckless dreamer, which is hard to see as anything but a weakness. Later it may prove that he is a real visionary and her cautiousness is to help refine his vision. After all, visionaries are only dreamers who do feasibility studies on their dreams.

After you have compared your lists, together list the similar character qualities in column 5, and the differences in column 6.

Column 5 Similarities	**Column 6** Differences
....	....
....	....
....	....
....	....
....	....
....	....

The similarities that appear on your lists may be an indication that you are well equipped as a couple for a particular occupation or ministry. But it is the differences which are the primary consideration in premarriage counselling.

Different is not wrong. It is different. We are interested in two types of differences: those which complement and those which require blending. If one partner is adventurous and the other is cautious this gives balance. They will have to move a bit towards each other but there is every indication that they will go through their married life fulfilling this role in their relationship. One will say, 'Let's go to the beach'. The other will check the weather report.

On the other hand, one may keep his or her flat like a tornado just ran through while the other is a 'neatnick'. These extremes do not give balance. There will have to be some blending in order for them to live together. They will have to agree on some type of standard. Chances are that Tornado Tony, desiring to have a testimony with outsiders, will admit his standards could be raised. But there is also a good chance that the burden of maintaining these new standards will fall on Nina the Neatnick. However, love will dictate that Tony at least pick up after himself.

Which of your differences will require blending?

. . . .

. . . .

What is the common ground you hope to find in these issues?

. . . .

. . . .

What major differences do you have, as a couple, that you could see causing real problems in marriage? How will you deal with them?

. . . .

. . . .

. . . .

Further reading

Dave and Joyce Ames, *Second Honeymoon* (Kingsway), Chapter 14.
Ed Wheat, *Love Life for Every Married Couple* (Marshalls), Chapter 11.

MATURITY IS:

Knowing that God is more committed to my character than my comfort.

John 16:33: 'I have told you these things, so that in me you may have peace. In this world you will have trouble. But take heart! I have overcome the world.'

4
Expectations and Negotiations

'Have you given any thought to dinner?'

Now that we have laid a foundation of general Christian concepts involved in marriage, it may be good to look at some of the specific expectations each of you, as prospective marriage partners, have for your marriage, your marriage partner and the way you intend to function in that marriage.

Expectations are what we consider to be reasonable behaviour, performance or decisions under a given set of circumstances. However, it is a fact of life that what is considered reasonable is the product of our experience and therefore varies from person to person. Consequently we do not dare assume that our partner will share our expectations in each situation.

Once you have discussed your expectations, you can use your areas of agreement to formulate objectives which will give purpose and direction to your relationship.

Objectives, in this instance then, are agreed expectations which will become a part of our value system giving direction to future decisions.

We would like you to use your expectations and the resultant negotiations as a basis for stating some of the objectives you hope to use for direction in your marriage. Hopefully, as you complete the chapters on more specific issues, you will be impressed to add other objectives for your marriage. Then, possibly, you will be able to develop some goals that will assure you attain those purposes.

For instance, the last chapter may have inspired you to make some very definite statements based on things your parents did or did not do in their marriage. So you may decide on a statement such as, 'We intend never to buy any item on HP'. This is a clearly-stated objective that is a feasible and practical way of dealing with finances. However, the statement also lacks any structure to be activated. It tells you what you want to avoid but not how you intend doing it. It is a bit like running a race with no starting or finishing lines.

Goals are a necessary element in realising our objectives. They consist of a clearly stated objective, which is feasible and practical, stated in terms of quantity when applicable and achievable in a definite time period.

An objective to stay out of debt will require many goals, eg, *We will establish an emergency back-up account of £300 before the wedding.* That will help insure you do not go into debt due to unforeseen, but inevitable, emergencies. *We will have sufficient to purchase a new car by our fifth anniversary.* That could go a long way towards avoiding car payments.

Developing specific goals to implement your objectives is not necessary and may not be practical at this point, but you will need to do that eventually. It is, however, very important that you share your expectations and develop the objectives necessary to guide you along the journey.

This exercise will take some thought and time on your part. Write twenty expectations you will have of your fiancé and/or your relationship when you are married. These can be simple or elaborate. For example, 'We should be involved in, and committed to our local church'.

When you both have completed your list, exchange with your partner. As you examine your partner's expectations, make a notation as to how you feel about it next to the number using the following codes:
Tick the expectations which will give you no problems.
Mark a D for difficulty if you think that expectation will cause you some difficulty. You may wish to use something such as ED for extreme difficulty.

Then negotiate on the items which cause any difficulty. For instance, a man may expect to have Saturdays to be off fishing with his mates. But his fiancée may think that all time not allocated to necessities such as work should be spent together. She may consider it rather selfish of him to want to reserve one day a week for his own personal pleasure. The issue is not one of having to choose between a partner and a sport or hobby, but it may well be the choice between a partner and the complete freedom to please oneself. The issue will be the method of determining how free time is spent.

Once you have come to an agreement on an expectation, form it into an objective statement, eg, 'We will establish no precedent which caters mainly to the desires of one at the expense of the other'. This neither precludes his fishing nor guarantees it. In this particular instance it is ridiculous to think that a married man can never go off and do things which do not involve his wife. But it is equally ridiculous to assume he can conduct his life exactly the same after marriage as before.

Marriage means change and that is the reason for negotiation.

At the end of this chapter there is a list entitled 'Decision Areas of Marriage', to jog your memory as to specific expectations you may have. It is not necessary to deliberate on each one. Some may look beyond the scope of a couple who are not yet married. Sex would seem to be one, but you will be discussing this and hopefully doing a fair amount of reading on the subject. This will create a certain amount of expectation. Foreplay, for instance, can rightly be defined as an activity intended to culminate in sexual intercourse, which means an engaged couple should not have entered into this yet. However, you will also learn that a major cause of sexual dissatisfaction is allowing too little time for foreplay. A major advantage in developing satisfying sexual relations is being committed to doing it right. Consequently there is no topic that is off limits for discussion, even if a few are off limits for experimentation.

Expectations

These are the things I expect in marriage

1 ....
2 ....
3 ....
4 ....
5 ....
6 ....
7 ....
8 ....
9 ....
10 ....

Do not go on to fill in the objectives list until you and your partner have begun negotiations on your expectations. It will probably not be necessary to form an objective statement on all expectations, eg 'Opening presents on Christmas morning rather than Christmas eve' is not such a critical issue as decision-making or finances. However, it is a good discipline to bring your negotiations down to concise statements so that both have the same expectations.

The couple that aims at nothing usually hits it.

MARRIAGE OBJECTIVES

We Purpose to Live by the Following:

1 ....
2 ....
3 ....
4 ....
5 ....
6 ....
7 ....
8 ....
9 ....

10 ....

11 ....

12 ....

Are there any of your objectives which require some action this side of marriage? If so you will find it helpful to set some goals to give short-range guidance. Write down the objective on the list below then follow it with the immediate goals for the action required.

Goals that really help in attaining our purposes are:

clearly stated expectations
feasible and practical
stated in terms of quantity when applicable
achievable in a definite time period

Example

Objective: To stay out of debt.
Goal: To develop a £300 back-up account by 1 May next year.
Goal: To establish a budget for monthly spending prior to the wedding.

Decision Areas of Marriage

For verbalising expectations and setting goals

Home:
- Buy or rent
- Price range
- Style
- Location
- Decoration
- Size and layout

Car:
- Price range
- Size
- Style
- Maintenance

Finances
- HP—debt in general
- Savings
- Emergency fund size (back-up account)
- Tithe and other giving

Budgeting
Financial decisions
Who maintains the cheque-book?
Separate accounts

Career considerations:
His occupational objectives
Her occupational objectives
Sacrifices towards career
- Overtime—how much are we willing to invest?
- Moving house—how much would we tolerate?
- Child-minding—considering the amount of time our child spends with a minder for us both to have careers, is it acceptable?
- Preparation (education etc)—how much more are we prepared to invest?

Church:
Type—denomination
Size
Involvement

Ministry:
Use of the home (how much?)
Joint ministry
Type—lay ministry or occupational
- Evangelistic, preaching, discipling, teaching, counselling, organising and co-ordinating, administrative, youth work, service.

Communication:
Depth
Amount
Frequency

Romance:
Special times—Dinners
The theatre
Quiet evenings
Sex—Frequency
Foreplay
Technique
Contraception

Children:
Number
How soon
Discipline
Education
Working mother

Extended family:
Social involvement (holidays etc)
Financial involvement
Business involvement

Roles:

- Headship and submission
- Decision-making

House-keeping chores:

- House cleaning
- Cooking—
  - size of meals
  - type of meals
- Washing-up
- Gardening
- Lawn mowing
- Laundry
- Dustbin
- Home maintenance
- Decorating
- Weekly shopping

Recreation:

- Sports—Will it pull us together or apart?
- Hobbies—Can we afford it?
- Pastimes—How will it contribute to our goals?
- Holidays—Where, when, how much?
- Television—Own, rent, pass.

Further reading

Dave and Joyce Ames, *Second Honeymoon* (Kingsway), Chapter 6.
Ed Wheat, *Love Life for Every Married Couple* (Marshalls), Chapter 8.
Joyce Huggett, *Growing Into Love* (IVP) Chapters 4 and 5.

MATURITY IS:

Recognising that there is no freedom without responsibility, because there is no effect without a cause.

Proverbs 30:33: 'For as churning milk produces butter, and as twisting the nose produces blood, so stirring up anger produces strife.'

5

Leaving, Cleaving and Priorities

The definition of Christian marriage we are using is:

> **Two people committed to meeting each other's needs,**
> **desiring their partner to meet their needs,**
> **recognising that their partner will sometimes fail,**
> **but knowing that Christ will not.**

Let us look at the word 'commitment'. This is a concept designed by God. In Genesis 2:24 he says, 'For this reason a man will leave his father and mother and be united to his wife, and they will become one flesh.' This is a basic paraphrase of the entire Bible teaching on marriage. It addresses the priority, depth and even the physical oneness of this most intimate of all relationships.

The very idea that we should leave our parental home establishes the fact that this is a new and totally autonomous family unit. We are never free from our obligation to honour our parents, but certainly once we are married, we accomplish this from an entirely independent stance. Because of their age and familiarity with our strengths and weaknesses their counsel may often be of greater value than any other. But it still falls into the category of advice no matter how sound it may be.

There is no biblical basis for parents to interfere with this new family unit. The fact that the Bible uses such strong language regarding what has been our closest relationship—that with our parents—tells something else as well. It tells us that all lesser relationships must also be subordinated to the priority of this new relationship. If God intended that parents should not be permitted to come between a husband and a wife, then surely football pals or the darts team, the sports club, or any other activity should not be allowed to be an obstacle to this new relationship. Marriage is not an extension of single life with sexual and domestic services thrown in.

Married life would be a drudgery if it consisted only of leaving all that had previously become important to us. But leaving is only half the commitment. Leaving is simply to clear the decks for cleaving, which is a lifetime project.

'Cleaving can best be defined as being welded together.'

Cleaving can best be defined as being welded together. When things are glued together there is a foreign substance in between, but when things are welded, the two are melted, or fused, into one unit. If this cleaving or oneness is actually to occur, it must be activated by a commitment to intimacy, not just physical intimacy but spiritual and psychological intimacy as well. Intimacy cannot be attained without making one's self vulnerable. Intimacy is risky because as the other person discovers our weaknesses they could exploit them. Being vulnerable implies a risk, but it also implies trust. And there can be no oneness without trust. Leaving and cleaving affect each other. People who are not willing to leave their families, both physically and psychologically, have great difficulty in actually becoming one with their partners. One can be emotionally dependent on a parent, calling home daily, looking to them for decisions or allowing parents' wishes and desires to come before one's partner. There is also the temptation to remain financially dependent on parents.

Some Practical Steps

1 Would you consider that either of you have a tendency to be dependent on your own parents:
Emotionally ....
Spiritually ....
Financially? ....
Please explain any yes answers.

2 Cleaving and becoming one is to be in every area of our being—spiritual, psychological/emotional and physical. Give some examples of situations which will require more vulnerability in your relationship as a couple. ....

....

....

....

Occasionally in counselling situations one partner complains that the other frequently (or always) sides with their own parents against them. In most instances further questioning reveals this to be true. Generally this is the result of an intimidating or manipulating parent. However, the responsibility for the resultant problem cannot be blamed solely on an overbearing parent; there is also a marriage partner who is failing to stand firm on biblical priorities at the expense of his or her partner.

3 Have you any reason to believe that either set of parents might make demands on either partner which would make 'leaving' difficult?

....

Lovingly explain any yes answers. ....

....

....

....

....

4 Have you seen any evidence that you or your intended could have

difficulty responding appropriately to 'in-law interference'? ....
If you perceive this could be a problem perhaps the two of you could discuss a contingency plan to deal with this.
The first thing on your list should be a commitment to discuss the situation as soon as either one even suspects a problem.
Whatever you do next, by way of confronting the parent involved, must be under the influence of the fifth commandment, 'Honour your father and your mother', and Ephesians 4:15, 'speaking the truth in love'. (See also the chapter on communication regarding confrontation.)

Reliance on parents is not the only thing which causes problems in cleaving. A husband, for instance, may fail to realise that he has given his career or ministry a higher priority than his wife. She, however, will be acutely aware of it and this will be an obstacle to cleaving. Many of our counselling cases involve a lack of biblical priorities.

Life is never short of decisions—many are charged with emotion. But the fact that God has given principles and priorities helps us to cut through this veil of emotional haze with certainty that can only be attained from the Master's plan.

The diagram below is presented as a building structure designed to show us how God's priorities build on one another and support each other. The foundation of all our relationship priorities is our relationship with God.

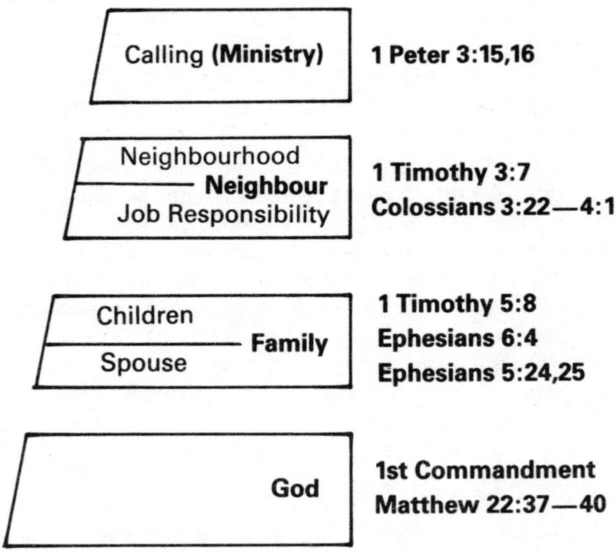

The next building block is our family priority in which our spouse actually takes precedence over the rest of the family. This could even be considered two separate blocks. It is difficult for some people to come to grips with the fact that children do not have a higher priority than partners, because some people feel that the purpose of marriage is producing children and therefore it should be the highest priority. However, a husband has no other relationship that he is told to love as Christ loved the church and gave himself up for her. And a wife has no other relationship where she is told to submit in everything as the church submits to Christ. And there is no other relationship in the Bible where the two become one.

The fact is that the relationship between a husband and wife is the highest form of loving commitment between human beings, and it is to serve as a model for children to understand what love and commitment consist of in God's economy. If children are allowed to come between the parents in this priority structure, they are being allowed to break the very model that God intended to teach them. However, children still take a higher priority than any outside relationship. As Paul states in 1 Timothy 5:8, 'If anyone does not provide for his relatives, and especially for his immediate family, he has denied the faith and is worse than an unbeliever.' This involves much more than mere physical requirements.

The next building block is our neighbour. This consists of all of the significant relationships in which God places us. For people who go out to work, undoubtedly their job responsibility is the most significant, for two reasons. First, they are involved in a witness for Christ approximately forty hours a week, to people who have an unusual opportunity to scrutinise their ethics, their lifestyle and their personal peace or lack of it. It is God's showcase in a secular society and a most significant ministry. Second, they are actually selling their time, consequently their integrity is being measured by how much value for money they give their employer. Paul has commented on this in several places. One such passage is Colossians 3:22–4:1, in which we are told to serve 'with sincerity of heart and reverence for the Lord'. The passage also includes instruction on management's responsibility to labour—they are to provide 'what is right and fair'.

We must have a proper testimony in our neighbourhood, we must actually be neighbourly. We should keep our house and garden in such a way that it is an asset to the neighbourhood. We want to be known as people who pay their bills on time and can be trusted and depended on for help if needed. How can we have a ministry that is really effective inside the church if we cannot live it outside the church? Paul told

Timothy that an overseer 'must...have a good reputation with outsiders, so that he will not fall into disgrace and into the devil's trap' (1 Timothy 3:7).

Each one of these blocks is a ministry. Secular employment is as sanctified as preaching if it is done 'as unto the Lord'.

On the foundation of these other priorities rests our called ministry—teaching, preaching or counselling etc. Some people have great difficulty with this because they have blurred the distinction between a personal relationship with God and a ministry calling. Having failed to make this distinction they are free to give their ministry calling a higher priority than their family. However, our relationship with God is comprised of our own personal devotional life, both prayer and Bible meditation, our willingness to live life in an attitude of communion with God and certainly in obedience to him and his priorities. We must remember that a God who can speak through donkeys and who maintains a vast army of angels does not require our services. He simply allows us a ministry calling.

The apostle Peter comes to grips with this priority structure as he addresses our ability to explain the gospel: 'Always be prepared to give an answer to everyone who asks you.' But he quickly goes on to say, 'keeping a clear conscience, so that those who speak maliciously against your good behaviour in Christ may be ashamed of their slander' (1 Peter 3:15, 16).

The credibility of our called ministry stands or falls with respect to the other priorities that God has laid out for us. As husbands and wives, we recognise that our first and most important ministry is to our partner, closely followed by our children. This does not mean that people with families cannot have ministry callings. There are so many needs that without a priority structure we would not know where to begin or when to say 'no'.

Some More Practical Steps

Ministry in the home never has a lower priority than that outside the home.

5 I agree/disagree with the priority structure offered in this chapter. List any reasons for disagreement.

....

....

....

6 What steps could you visualise taking to ensure your marriage relationship receives the proper priority?

....

....

7 What steps will you take to ensure that God receives his proper priority in your life as an individual once you become married and new demands are made on your time?

....

....

8 What ideas do you have of how you and your intended will continue to assure that God is the number one priority in your relationship?

....

....

....

9 What do you see as your main spiritual gift and how do you see ministering together as a couple?

....

....

Are there any further statements that you can add to your objectives on page 41?

Further reading

Dave and Joyce Ames, *Second Honeymoon* (Kingsway), Chapter 8.
Selwyn Hughes, *Marriage As God Intended* (Kingsway), Chapter 5.
Joyce Huggett, *Two Into One* (IVP), Chapter 5.
Joyce Huggett, *Marriage on the Mend* (Kingsway), Chapters 2 and 3.

MATURITY IS:

Recognising that it is not a commitment to self which brings happiness in life but rather a commitment to others.

Matthew 10:39: 'Whoever finds his life will lose it, and whoever loses his life for my sake will find it.'

6

Communication and Conflict

Communication is the vehicle of relationship—it provides the transport from one individual to another. A relationship is only as deep and as effective as its communication. We are all aware that there are various levels of communication. The number of levels is arbitrary, but it certainly is apparent that there is a very light, superficial, cliché level of communication that serves little more than to acknowledge the presence of another person. 'How are you?'—'I'm fine', and talk about the weather are designed to make another individual feel comfortable, to let them know that we are positively disposed towards them when we cannot think of anything more significant to say. This level of communication cannot do much to enhance a relationship because it is too non-committal.

A more serious level is exchanging facts, ideas and opinions, intellectual concepts or even discussing doctrine. Close friends and certainly married couples ought to be very familiar with the ideas and opinions held by their partner. One of the key functions of courtship is to find out where our prospective life-mate stands on a myriad of issues that could affect the relationship in the future. The intellectual stance that is taken by a friend on various issues of life should be understood because meaningful friendship is difficult between people who do not know, do not care about or cannot comprehend the other's thoughts or philosophy of life.

This does not mean that every doctor must marry a nurse and that a Greek professor should immediately set out to teach his bride Greek on their honeymoon, but partners do have the responsibility to educate each other in the basic rudiments of their profession so that when they begin to share their victories or challenges, the other will have at least a basic working knowledge to understand the story being told.

However, the level of conversation that really deepens and strengthens a relationship goes deeper than facts, ideas and opinions. There should be a fair amount of feeling-level conversation.

We are often attracted to another person by their physical appearance and sometimes by their ideas, opinions and goals. However, physical appearance and intellect are insufficient foundation for effective long-lasting relationships. Qualities such as unselfishness, sensitivity, honesty, and temperament would also be key factors in the total person. It would be nearer the mark to say we fall in love with the personality.

How do we discover a person's personality? It is mainly through what they verbalise as well as their facial expressions and body language. This is why we have chosen a mouth (on the following diagram) to represent the outgoing side of a personality; but this is only one side of the personality.

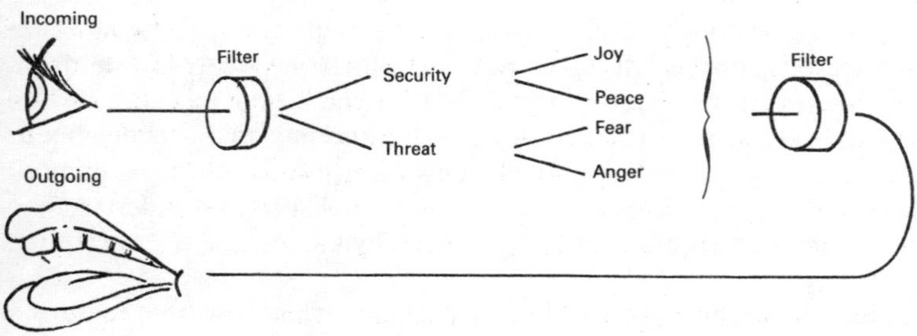

There is also an incoming side. It is equally important to understand the incoming side of a personality. Perception is the way a person actually sees life unfolding around him or herself. Every incident that occurs within our circle of awareness causes us to ask the question 'How does this affect me?'. This is a part of our survival instinct; it is healthy. We evaluate the incident in terms of our own security. Does it enhance or threaten our security or is it of no consequence to us?

Depending upon this determination, we develop appropriate emotional responses. If it enhances our security we feel things like joy and peace. If it threatens our security we feel things like fear or anger. Consequently we frequently have an emotional response to this question, 'How does it affect me?'. However, we can see by the diagram it is not just a straight shot from the eyeball into the security judgement. There is a filter that all these experiences must go through.

This filter is made up of everything that has ever happened in our life, plus our basic temperament. It has the greatest influence on the security judgement. The reason it is important to share feelings is that the sharing of emotions gives an insight to the fabric and function of the filter. **When we know how someone's filter functions we are more effective at loving them in a way that they will perceive as love.** We also know how deeply a person is committed to certain intellectual concepts.

Judson Swiahart's book *How Do You Say I Love You?*[1] lists many different 'languages' of love that people speak and understand. He lists expression of love through words, touch, spending time together, providing material needs and many others. Individuals vary in the way they perceive love. Much of this is due largely to the construction of their filter. Let us face it, it helps to know a person to give an effective compliment, or constructive criticism. Answering questions such as 'How do you like my new suit?' or 'Is the pie I just baked okay?' often requires knowledge of the other person's filter to do justice to the situation.

It is obvious that the more we are aware of the feelings, the more we understand about the filter and the better placed we are to minister to an individual's needs. This is why it is very important to share on the feeling level. We are required to love one another, love our neighbour and to love our marriage partner. This means doing the right thing to meet their needs. This can be best accomplished by understanding exactly how different issues are perceived by the one we are attempting to love.

The reason this information is not readily available is that there is a second filter. Once we have arrived at peace, joy, fear or anger, etc, we have somewhat of a choice about what we do with it. The first filter sends a signal to the second filter telling it how much to allow to go through to the outgoing side of our personality. This rear filter serves a very good purpose. It is the device which allows us to 'speak the truth in love'; be judicious about how we answer others in order not to offend them.

[1] Judson Swiahart, *How Do You Say I Love You?* (Kingsway Publications, 1978).

Unfortunately we also use it strategically with regard to ourselves, often in an overprotective way, which also insulates us from having our needs met by those around us. After all if we say, 'I didn't appreciate that remark,' that tells the world something about us, and we may perceive that it is unwise to let people know that the remark disturbs us at all so we do not share our feelings. It may be we are afraid that if they understood our needs they might use that information in some way to exploit us.

This is where vulnerability comes in. There can be no real intimacy without risk, but it is difficult to establish trust without risk to demonstrate it. We must also remember that it affirms the worth of our partner when we share the things we would not consider prudent to share with others. Or as Dr Ed Wheat puts it in *Love Life for Every Married Couple*, 'If you are afraid to try it because you are afraid you will be hurt, consider this: the risk of pain is always the price of life.'[1]

[1] Ed Wheat, *Love Life for Every Married Couple* (Marshalls, 1984), p 83.

There are two basic rules about sharing feelings. The first is, we cannot blame feelings on the other person. It is not right to share feelings in a sentence such as 'You make me feel...' because in actuality the other person does not make us feel this way. Our filter is more to blame than the other person. He or she is doing a certain thing and we interpret it in a certain way which elicits a given emotion.

What so often happens is that we do not share feelings till finally the back filter gets overloaded and we literally blow a hole through it sending forth a gush of accusations which are totally counter-productive. This is why Matthew 18:15 gives the admonition that if our brother sins against us we should go to the brother and show him his fault. This is opposed to simply 'stifling our emotions' until we can stifle no more and we blow our filter out and say things for which we are sorry.

The second rule is not to condemn another person's feelings when they share them. It is very easy when someone finally opens their filter sufficiently to say 'I feel angry about such and such' or 'I feel fearful' to turn around and tell them why a Christian should not feel that way. 'Don't you know God has not given you the spirit of fear but of love and a sound mind?'

Violating either one of these rules will make feeling-level conversation difficult or non-existent. The only thing that will be acceptable from that point is intellectual sharing. Intellectual sharing is interesting but not very romantic.

James 1:19 says, 'Everyone should be quick to listen, slow to speak and slow to become angry'. Communication problems arise because we do not listen. We are too preoccupied with our own thoughts to listen for understanding. Yet, how well we listen communicates how interested we are in the relationship.

Some Practical Steps

1 Are you a good listener? On a rating of 1 to 10 score your ability as a listener. ☐

2 How would you rate your partner? ☐

3 What are your feelings about sharing your inner thoughts, attitudes and emotions with your intended?

....

....

....

4 When bringing up areas of disagreement, does your partner sometimes attack with 'you' statements, such as 'You have made us late again'. If the answer is yes, give some examples and how you would rather hear them phrased.

....

....

....

5 'I'm encouraged to be more open and vulnerable with you when you...' ....

....

....

....

Resolving Conflict

For some engaged couples it is difficult to imagine ever having a conflict, while others have already experienced quite a few. The term 'conflict' need not necessarily be limited to 'a right old barney'. It could be simply a difference of opinion where conflicting views bring us to an impasse. Whether or not we have a right old barney depends on how it is handled.

Our temperament has a lot to do with the way we naturally handle conflicts. This ranges all the way from a peace-at-any-price avoidance of anything that even looks like a conflict, to seeing a conflict as a sporting competition with one more opportunity to win. Others think the mature way to deal with conflict is to compromise. It is not nearly as important to identify our wrong ways of dealing with conflict as it is to learn how to resolve them.

One of the most important things to learn regarding conflict is to accept it as one of the normal challenges of life. It is important to remember that when two people agree on everything, one of them is redundant. God does not put people together who think alike on every issue. It is not in God's best interest or ours that we should agree on everything, but that we should complement and complete one another.

Second, it is a part of God's character development curriculum. He is in the business of conforming us to the image of his Son, and learning to handle conflict is a part of the spiritual maturity process.

Differences of opinion do not limit themselves to discussions. They often appear in the form of socks and underwear left on the bedroom floor, lawn-mower left out in the rain, toilet seat left up, or bank account overdrawn. These dilemmas may even present themselves shortly after a long policy discussion when both parties have agreed on the proper procedure. This could cause the offended party to feel they have been grievously and wantonly sinned against.

Some newly-weds find it beneficial to have one small piece of Romans 12:21 ready to hand as an emergency procedure: **'Overcome evil with good.'** Attached to this should be four short reasons to do so:

1 I am committed to God.
2 I am committed to my partner.
3 I know my partner is committed to God.
4 I know my partner is committed to me.

A wife who is naturally neat could not imagine somebody leaving dirty clothes strewn around the bedroom, especially after having discussed it. Therefore it is easy to assume that this must be a deliberate, callous attempt to inflict hurt. Any man who would do this is certainly not committed to her, could not possibly be committed to godliness, therefore the whole basis of their relationship is shattered.

We do not believe that anyone actually consciously thinks this way, but when we have helped people work through their emotions, in retrospect, that is what it actually boils down to.

Few of us are comfortable with confrontations because they frequently lead to full-fledged blow-ups. However Matthew 18:15, cited earlier, tells us that is our responsibility when things are going wrong. Let us assume you have made an agreement not to purchase anything on HP. What should you do when your partner comes in with a £500 stereo purchased on the Visa card, and you know that there are no funds to pay the bill when it arrives—ignore it? It is at this point that a right heart attitude would benefit greatly from an intelligent technique.

The first thing to remember is that if we speak in terms of 'I' and 'me', rather than 'you', we run less danger of erecting barriers on the other side. Statements such as 'I have a problem I think you can help me with' are infinitely more effective than 'You've done it again,' or 'Why do you always clutter?'

The next thing is to assure that the statement being made is a description of the offensive behaviour and not the offender's character. In Parliament one may say 'The right honourable gentleman has misled the house,' but one may not say 'The right honourable gentleman is a liar'. This would be a very effective rule in most households.

Be prepared to listen once you have introduced the problem. Give the other person the opportunity to present their reasoning.

Demonstrate careful consideration of the facts. Considering the ideas of others affirms their personal worth. Rejecting ideas out of hand implies personal rejection. Remember your ideas may have a serious flaw. It may be a chance to avoid a mistake and those painful words 'I tried to warn you.'

Look for areas of agreement and concentrate on these before addressing areas of disagreement.

If possible pray together for God's wisdom. 'But the wisdom that comes from heaven is first of all pure; then peace-loving, considerate, submissive, full of mercy and good fruit, impartial and sincere' (James 3:17).

Remember you cannot receive a confrontation and give one at the same time. We are severely tempted when receiving a confrontation to imply that the pot is calling the kettle black, which is another way of saying 'you have no right to speak to me until you are perfect yourself'.

God is not as interested in getting us through a conflict as he is in how we respond to it. He is more committed to our character than our comfort. He is using your partner as divine sandpaper to take off the rough edges.

Love requires vulnerability, being vulnerable enough to share weaknesses or confront our partner over problem issues.

Some More Practical Steps

1 How do you normally respond to conflict situations such as differences of opinions, or when your goals clash with another? Are you out to win? Do you withdraw? Do you become a martyr? Give in? Compromise? Attempt to resolve the conflict?

. . . .

. . . .

2 What conflicts have you had with your intended in the past and how did you (as an individual) handle them?

. . . .

. . . .

. . . .

. . . .

3 In what ways can you improve your method of handling conflicts?

. . . .

. . . .

. . . .

. . . .

4 What are the types of issues that you can 'agree to disagree' on without affecting the quality of relationship?

. . . .

. . . .

. . . .

. . . .

5 How might you incorporate the principle of Ephesians 4:26–27, 'Do not let the sun go down while you are still angry, and do not give the devil a foothold', into a goal for your marriage?

. . . .

. . . .

. . . .

6 Do you foresee the way you as a couple handle conflict affecting your ability to make decisions together?

. . . .

Are there any further statements that you can add to your objectives on page 41?

Further reading

Dave and Joyce Ames, *Second Honeymoon* (Kingsway), Chapter 4.
Joyce Huggett, *Marriage on the Mend* (Kingsway), Chapter 4.
Joyce Huggett, *Two Into One* (IVP), Chapter 3.
Selwyn Hughes, *Marriage As God Intended* (Kingsway), Chapter 3.
Ian and Ruth Coffey, *Marriage—the Early Years* (Kingsway), Chapter 4.

MATURITY IS:

Being quicker to affirm than to condemn.

Ephesians 4:29: 'Do not let any unwholesome talk come out of your mouths, but only what is helpful for building others up according to their needs, that it may benefit those who listen.'

7

Roles and Decisions

Christianity is at odds with the world in almost every sphere of life. Family roles are no exception. The very idea that the family should have any role structure is out of phase with the spirit of the age. However, the rebellion against this concept has had one positive effect. It has forced the church to make a much greater distinction between traditional cultural roles and biblical responsibilities.

Headship and submission are caricatured by the world as authoritarian and being a doormat. Insecure Christian men feeling threatened have fallen back on the Scriptures with authoritarian tunnel vision, while Christian women are learning Greek and Hebrew in order to find a loophole to invalidate this 'yoke of bondage'.

The first myth in the caricature is that authority implies superiority and submission inferiority. This is an easy trap to fall into because humans quite naturally promote people on the basis of superior performance. However, there is no evidence in the Bible that God invests authority in an individual because that individual is in any way superior. God is not looking for ability, but availability. He is not looking for people who can make decisions for him, but people through whom he can implement his decisions.

Moses, for instance, was a whimpering mass of inferiority as God began to commission him at the burning bush. David had done absolutely nothing to earn his spurs when Samuel anointed him. Peter was famous for nothing besides denying the Lord and putting his foot in his mouth up to the kneecap on several occasions, but he was chosen. God knew their hearts and knew they were willing to make all that they had totally available to him.

'Honestly God, if you had seen my performance reports for the last forty years you would not be offering me this position.'

Nathan, on the other hand, we are sure, did not feel inferior as he served under David's rule and was not the least bit reticent about confronting him with his sin. Submission in no way equates to inferiority.

With our modern use of words it is possible to look at God's statement in Genesis 2:18—'It is not good for the man to be alone. I will make a helper suitable for him'—and conclude that Eve was a junior assistant. However, this is easily corrected when it is pointed out that the Bible refers to God, himself, as a helper. The same Hebrew word for helper used in connection with Eve is used in Deuteronomy 33:29 when God is described to Israel as their shield and *helper*, and in Psalm 121:1, 'I lift up my eyes to the hills—where does my *help* come from? My *help* comes from the Lord, the Maker of heaven and earth.' All are the same Hebrew word.

Once we have ruled out the secular notion that authority implies superiority, we can then get it back into perspective as simply a necessary tool in executing responsibility. Regardless of all the toing and froing in Christian periodicals regarding women in leadership roles, no one has ever come up with anything remotely convincing which would relieve husbands from the responsibility for the direction of their families. The fact that husbands are charged with this responsibility is not negotiable. They do not have to desire it, apply for it, or be qualified for it. God says it is theirs whether they want it or not.

When one considers that the family is the basic unit of society, it is not surprising to find it also embodies some very logical management considerations as well. It would seem God had a choice: a fifty/fifty partnership, or to pick one sex to be the partner held responsible through all generations. Both options are open to abuse. Both are only as successful as our ability to set aside our personal agenda in favour of the family unit. However, since it is obvious that human society could never advance without some sort of leadership structure, what makes us think the family, society's basic unit, would be any less an anarchy with equal responsibility?

The biblical position on family structure definitely includes male headship. However, there is more to marriage than family structure. One of the objectives is that the two become one. Therefore it is equally important to remember that when two people are committed to investing their lives in each other, the actual outworking of this structure on a day-to-day basis will be much more a partnership. Headship becomes obscured by partnership because in marriage partnership is the aim. Headship is only a tool and one that is used sensitively and less frequently as the goal of oneness nears (although there are always some who are more enamoured with the tools than the results).

Probably the most common area for abuse of headship is the decision-making process. The most glaring sin is the failure of husbands adequately to interact with their wives' ideas, and the ultimate wrongheadedness of not consulting her in the first place. This latter stems from the notion 'I am in charge—therefore I make the decisions'. Not only does this demonstrate a poor commitment to oneness, it is also very poor leadership technique. In fact it is these abuses that have provided the ammunition to bring the entire concept of headship into disrepute.

First, we need to remember that as a reflection of God, Adam was somewhat incomplete. 'So God created man in his own image, in the image of God he created him; male and female he created them' (Genesis 1:27). Not all of the attributes of God that he intended to pass along to the human race were present in Adam, eg God has a mother's heart.

Second, if leadership in God's economy is not given on a basis of superiority then there is no reason to assume that the husband is the best equipped to make a given decision. His partner may be much more knowledgeable.

Third, it is also reasonable to assume that if there is some quality in Eve which completes Adam, that she is different and that this difference in focus can frequently add a valuable insight to the decision-making process.

Fourth, 'two heads *are* better than one'. The debate which may ensue from involving another person in a decision may at times seem to complicate things, but more often than not it adds to the validity of the decision.

The marriage ceremony is not a process whereby a wife abdicates her role in the decision-making process, nor does it give husbands the right to unilateral decisions. In fact, just the opposite is true. Where partners have had only their own opinion to consider, they are now compelled by their new circumstances to seek counsel from each other. Proverbs 13:10 tells us 'Pride only breeds quarrels, but wisdom is found in those who take advice', and for some this may be the first experience in considering opinions other than their own.

In a survey conducted in 1987 among 4,500 women, 77 per cent cited as their major cause of anger, 'He doesn't listen'. This is obviously where the lack of leadership skills and abuse of headship most frequently surfaces. No one feels they are a team member, much less a partner, if decisions are continually made without their consultation.

Listening, alone, is not sufficient. Partners must interact with each other's ideas. We find that frequently when a husband does listen, he does little to indicate to his wife that he is actually considering her input. Consequently it is necessary for him to provide her with feedback so that she is aware that her opinion is duly considered. This is sometimes reversed; wives are not always good listeners.

Ephesians 5:21 tells us to 'Submit to one another out of reverence for Christ' and we feel that this is implemented when one partner listens respectfully to the other's opinion and demonstrates consideration for it. This means that we are seen to be *thinking with* our partner rather than *thinking against* them.

As couples live together over a period of years they will find more and more areas where decisions can be made without consultation because they will understand a lot of each other's interests and desires.

Thinking With　　　　　Thinking Against

'I think that block would do better over here.'

But even this can be dangerous because we are all growing, changing humans who do not want to be 'taken for granted'.

When decisions are continually made with respectful consultation it is very seldom that authority is ever actually involved. It is only when all the options have been considered, all the ideas have been exchanged and the husband still considers his plan to be more appropriate that both he and his partner understand he has the responsibility to follow that plan prayerfully. He does so believing that if, in the long run, it is not the best for all concerned God will intervene through circumstances or additional information.

This happened to us a few years back. After two years of searching we found a house that seemed to meet all of our requirements. It seemed a logical choice. One of us was uneasy, even though they were not able to explain why, but they were not the one with final responsibility. We prayerfully proceeded with the purchasing process, only to have the property survey reveal a £5,000 defect. The repair would have taken us over our budget so we saw this as God's way to close the door. He provided a better place, which the uneasy partner did not even want to look at, but admits could not be better.

Actually when you consider that particular kind of situation, what type of person would, in a crucial decision, knowing he was charged with the responsibility for the direction of his family, say 'I consider my plan to be the most effective, but we'll do it your way to keep peace'? I think we would all find that irresponsible.

Authority was never given for the benefit of the person in authority, but only as a tool to serve those under that authority.

The Bible sees leadership as synonymous with servanthood. 'Jesus called them together and said, "You know that the rulers of the Gentiles lord it over them, and their high officials exercise authority over them. Not so with you. Instead, whoever wants to become great among you must be your servant, and whoever wants to be first must be your slave—just as the Son of Man did not come to be served, but to serve, and to give his life as a ransom for many" ' (Matthew 20:25–28).

Biblical leadership is an act of love, because it has the long-range goal of doing the best for those being led.

Some Practical Steps

1 Do you see leadership primarily as a relationship skill or the exercise of authority? Explain.

....

....

....

....

2 What are your thoughts about equality of the sexes?

....

....

....

....

3 Do you agree with the above narrative that submission in no way implies inferiority? See John 5:19, 30, 6:38, 1 Corinthians 11:3 and Philippians 2:5–8.

....

Regardless of our commitment to joint decision-making most of us will find that there are many decisions where we feel we lack either sufficient interest or qualification and are perfectly happy to leave those decisions to our partner, eg many men would feel primarily responsible for choosing a car but would prefer their wives to pick out the furniture, decorations and plan the kitchen. That is not true in our home. We have an equal interest in home decoration and our car is chosen on the basis of cost, economy, safety and comfort, all of which is easily understood by both of us. That is neither right or wrong; we both have an interest and both want to be in on the decision. There are still areas where we tend to look at the other as 'the resident expert', or at least more expert than we consider ourself to be.

It should be pointed out that simply deciding who decides is a decision and should be a joint one. It is a decision that may require continual revision. Additionally, it is wise to keep our partner apprised of decisions being made, if for no other reason than avoiding them feeling left out. Also some decisions are multiple. A decision to purchase new curtains is more than a matter of taste; it is also a financial decision.

4 Who would you expect to have the major input into the decision-making process in the following areas? Mark an 'E' to indicate those issues which you think demand equal involvement and use your partner's initials to indicate areas where you would expect them to have the major input.

Choosing a house ____ Choosing furniture ____
Choosing curtains ____ Choosing a car ____
Choosing a lawn-mower ____ Planning a garden ____
Choosing a church ____ Church involvement ____
Entertaining ____ Choosing a school for the children or selecting a neighbourhood with that in mind ____

Add any other areas that come to your mind.

....

....

5 Write down what you consider would be the effect of leadership without respect by the leader for those being led.

....

....

6 Write what you consider to be the relationship between respect and submission.

....

....

....

....

....

7 Comment on the relationship between servanthood and leadership.

....

. . . .

. . . .

. . . .

8 The following household tasks are generally assigned purely on a cultural basis. Considering your own ability, experience and anticipated schedule contrasted with that of your partner, tick the tasks you would feel the most comfortable with.

Washing-up ☐	Laundry ☐	Lawn care ☐
Gardening ☐	Bathing children ☐	Paying bills ☐
Car care ☐	Keeping accounts ☐	Cooking ☐
Home maintenance ☐	House cleaning ☐	Painting ☐
Wall papering ☐	Dustbin ☐	Changing nappies ☐

Men. You are about to assume a place of responsibility which requires giving yourself up for your wife as per Ephesians 5:25–33. Surely God is more aware than any of us that marriage involves two basically selfish sinners in a commitment to each other. Therefore he realises that there will be times when this command will seem unfair, uncomfortable and unreasonable.

9 How do you see this will affect your marriage relationship?

. . . .

. . . .

. . . .

10 How will this affect you personally?

. . . .

. . . .

. . . .

Women. Most people would say that respect is something that must be earned. However, since the Ephesians 5:33 statement 'and the wife must respect her husband' has no clause such as 'If he deserves it', we must conclude that there is a certain heart attitude she is responsible for. It would seem that God expects her efforts towards meeting her partner's needs to be channelled into this attitude of respect, even though there will obviously be times when it will be difficult.

11 How do you see this will benefit your marriage relationship?

. . . .

. . . .

. . . .

12 How do you see this will benefit you as a person?

. . . .

. . . .

. . . .

For You Were Truly a Man

At times Lord I feel like an object
With limited value to some
Not because that's how you would want it
But because it's the way it's become.
When I see how you treated woman
Made them a sure part of your plan
It makes me feel like a woman
For you were truly a man.

You met a Samaritan woman
Were willing to put aside race
You offered her living water
Not to trick her but show her your grace
Your way was to make her realistic
To face up to what was your plan
You treated her gently not harshly
For you were truly a man.

One day you saw a loose woman
Aggressive, bound and disturbed
You freed her from Satan's tight bondage
Her spirit soared free like a bird.
She loved you completely not partly
Stayed close while the menfolk all ran
You made her feel like a woman
For you were truly a man.

As you walked one day in the temple
The Pharisees came with a grin
Brought a woman they'd caught in adultery
And stood her before you in sin.
They asked you a question to trap you
You bent down and wrote in the sand
You left her complete as a woman
For you were truly a man.

My heart overflows with a freedom
I find it so hard to express
You've raised me to sit in high places
In spite of my doubts you still bless
You tenderly chasten and mould me
Uphold me by your nail pierced hand
You made me completely a woman
For you were truly a man.

Mary-Jo Taylor

Are there any further statements that you can add to your objectives on page 41?

Further reading

Dave and Joyce Ames, *Second Honeymoon* (Kingsway), Chapters 6, 7 and 9.
Ed Wheat, *Love Life for Every Married Couple* (Marshalls), Chapter 13.
Joyce Huggett, *Marriage on the Mend* (Kingsway), Chapters 9 and 10.

MATURITY IS:

Understanding that my own limited knowledge need not be a limiting factor.

Proverbs 15:22: 'Plans fail for lack of counsel, but with many advisers they succeed.'

8

Self in Marriage

After we have talked about selfishness and family priorities, it would seem logical to wonder where self fits into the whole scheme of things. Psychologist Lawrence Crabb, in his excellent book *The Marriage Builder*,[1] states that in addition to needs for food, clothing and shelter, we also have a need for love and significance. This seems to be one area where the Bible, psychology and common sense are all in agreement. But only the Bible assures us that both of these needs are met in Christ.

It is a natural tendency to want to be loved, because that makes us feel of worth, just as it is a natural tendency to achieve in order to gain personal significance. Unfortunately, the extent to which we are loved, our degree of significance and the way we perceive it are different things.

Many people who are admired for their career success and professional expertise feel a failure. And we have counselled many women who were both mentally bright and physically beautiful, whose personal assessment was that they were stupid and ugly. A newspaper interview with the very successful American actress Brook Shields quoted her as saying that she constantly worries 'that I'm not pretty enough, that I'm too fat, that I'm not smart enough and that I'm not a good enough actress'.

The reason these worries pose such a problem in marriage relationships is that if we feel insignificant we assume we are unworthy of love and are afraid of the vulnerability that comes with complete openness and honesty. Some years ago a man named John Powell wrote a book

[1] Lawrence Crabb, *The Marriage Builder* (NavPress, 1987), Chapter 2.

entitled *Why Am I Afraid To Tell You Who I Am?* [1] Before he finished writing the book, someone gave him an answer to the question. 'I am afraid to tell you who I am, because if I tell you who I am you may not like who I am and it is all that I have.' [1]

In other words, the very fact that we do not consider we are worth loving causes us to put up barriers that ensure people will not have the opportunity to love us. The second major problem is that people who do not consider that these needs have been met continually manipulate others to meet them. Rather than achieving for the sheer stimulation, or intrinsic worth of the achievement, they are driven in a never-ending competition 'to be someone'. They can easily become workaholics, name droppers, gossips and braggarts.

Others who do not feel loved frequently become very insular, or create situations which cause others to feel sorry for them, or even guilty. The common tendency of all of these people is to be so concerned with manipulating others to meet their needs that they have no time to minister to their partner's needs.

The good news is that these needs are met in Christ. 1 John 3:16 tells us that we only know what love is because 'Jesus Christ laid down his life for us'. 1 John 3:1 says, 'How great is the love the Father has lavished on us, that we should be called children of God! And that is what we are!'

The reason we know that God recognises this dimension in the human personality is that he goes to such great lengths to make it very clear that he loves us, and one of his primary commands to us is that we

[1] John Powell, *Why Am I Afraid To Tell You Who I Am?* (Fontana Books: London, 1969), p 12.

must love one another. 1 John 3:16 goes on to say, 'And we ought to lay down our lives for our brothers.' God also created us to have significance. He has given each one of us a ministry. Ephesians 2:10 states, 'For we are God's workmanship, created in Christ Jesus to do good works, which God prepared in advance for us to do.' Each one of us has been called into ministry with the God of the universe. This is significant. In 1 Corinthians 12 Paul talks about a 'body'. He does not talk about important jobs and unimportant jobs. Instead he talks about jobs which each have significance and depend upon each other.

Paul also warns that there is no way we can compare our significance with that of anyone else. There is no way we can measure ourselves, or the actual eternal worth that we have by comparing ourselves. In 2 Corinthians 10:12 he says, 'We do not dare to classify or compare ourselves with some who commend themselves. When they measure themselves by themselves and compare themselves with themselves, they are not wise.'

We are constantly reminded that we cannot use the visible indicators as value assessments. Inferior and superior are relative standards and have no place in the biblical vocabulary regarding the worth of a person.

We frequently fall victim to this relative mentality because we live in a society that has nothing else by which to determine ethics, values or the worth of a person. Consequently everything is relative.

The easiest way to avoid this pitfall is to separate human conduct into behaviour and performance. Behaviour, for this purpose, has to do with the ethics of our actions, the rightness or wrongness of them. And performance has to do with our skill and ability.

Behaviour is never determined on a relative basis. We stand either not guilty or condemned before a righteous God and are never excused or condemned because our actions fall above or below group expectations. For instance, sexual promiscuity is a sin according to the Bible, but it is not considered a sin by a sexually promiscuous society. One who is less promiscuous in a promiscuous society is not excused before God. He is still guilty because he has violated God's law. One who is not promiscuous at all is not superior. He is simply not guilty of promiscuity.

God holds us responsible for our actions as a part of his character development programme. He is developing the character of Christ in our lives and as a result he is holding us responsible for our behaviour. However, he even makes a way to deal with wrong behaviour. He says in 1 John 1:9, 'If we confess our sins, he is faithful and just and will forgive us our sins and purify us from all unrighteousness.'

Performance, on the other hand, can definitely be measured on a relative basis. The person who crosses the finish line first in a race has definitely had the most superior performance that day. Preaching sermons can be rated on a performance basis: is the material good, does it flow logically, does the speaker have a good command of the language, and is he holding people's attention? Points could be allowed for each quality, and the most superior performance could be determined. But that would not explain why some of the sermons that have had the greatest impact on us have not necessarily been high on the performance scale. God is sovereign, and he is able to give value to the performance according to his purposes. He takes what we make available to him and makes out of it what he will.

The eternal significance of our performance is difficult, if not impossible, to determine this side of glory, but we know that there is a correlation between that significance and our commitment to God and his purposes. Testimonies lived out in daily life may frequently have a greater impact for eternity than many a well-delivered sermon. If men and women are faithful to do what God has called them to do and to serve where God has called them to serve, they have a genuinely significant ministry. A taxi driver, teacher or taxidermist need not feel inferior to anyone with a high profile, high rating, high budget ministry. Many of these leave a very big question mark as to their eternal significance. However, the understanding of significance within the individual believer must be based on a scriptural footing, rather than the visible indicators. We are told to 'fix our eyes not on what is seen, but on what is unseen. For what is seen is temporary, but what is unseen is eternal' (2 Corinthians 4:18).

The important thing in dealing with our self-image is that we recognise that we are different creatures with different skills and abilities, and that we have a very realistic idea of what our skills and inabilities actually are. This is necessary to make sure we are functioning in a realistic way, that we are not kidding ourselves that we have abilities that we do not, but more importantly, to ensure we are not allowing our inabilities to nullify our abilities.

In Romans 12:3 Paul says, 'For by the grace given me I say to every one of you: Do not think of yourself more highly than you ought, but rather think of yourself with sober judgment, in accordance with the measure of faith God has given you.' This is a call for an accurate self-appraisal, which in turn gives the opportunity to practise a very well-known management technique—capitalise on your strengths and staff to your weaknesses.

To capitalise on one's strengths is a fairly self-evident statement. Staffing to weaknesses may be a little more ambiguous. In a business or management sense it means that when an individual or a company identifies weaknesses, they hire staff or let contracts to handle those jobs that they cannot handle themselves.

However, in everyday life it is not always feasible to think of hiring someone. The person who has difficulty with simple accounting cannot always afford to have someone keep his cheque-book up to date. And the person who is not clever with his hands cannot always afford to hire someone to put shelves up in his larder. But we can help one another. This is especially true as married couples.

We can help others identify strengths. We can encourage them in these gifts and enhance them. Frequently we find that we have the ability to staff to our partner's weaknesses. For instance I (Dave) am dyslexic, which means I am an atrocious speller. Also, I am not a typist and I would never have written my first book if I did not know that Joyce was able and willing to decipher my handwriting, unsnarl my spelling and type the manuscript. She felt I had something to say, a strength, and she was willing to staff to my weaknesses to make sure that it was said.

We have a need for love and a need for significance and God meets both of these needs, sometimes directly and sometimes indirectly, through others around us, mainly our partners. But we must remember that our partner is the agent of that love and not the source of it. If we look at our partner as the source of that love we put too much pressure on them.

No one person can meet all our needs. The world's response to this is a 'Dr Zhivago mentality', which is 'if one lover can't meet my needs I will have two'. As Christians, the awareness that Christ is the source of our love and significance frees us to serve our partner and staff to their weaknesses to help them become the man or woman God intended them to be.

Human worth cannot be found apart from God

An Accurate Self-appraisal

The lists in Chapter 3 will provide you with a lot of ready-made ideas for this chapter, but think hard before you just copy them over. Be sure that you are making a distinction between the instructions and intent of that chapter and this one.

What are your assets? Include such items as concern for others; being slow to anger; a willingness to serve. Are you kind, considerate, easy-going, or out-going? Are you selfless, or sensitive? Are you a jolly person; do you have a good sense of humour? Are you a hard worker; are you loyal, trustworthy or faithful? These are all assets which not everyone has and can help you in achieving your goals.

Are you a creative person? Do you have specific skills, such as writing, typing, bookkeeping, administration in general? Are you a fast reader with the ability to retain the key points? Are you a competent carpenter, plumber, welder, mechanic? Do you have gifts such as music, or preaching, or teaching or even story-telling? Are you athletic or physically strong? Are you forceful; are you goal oriented? Do you have perseverance?

These are merely suggestions, only a fraction of the positive qualities which could be listed on this work sheet.

What are your liabilities? What are your negative qualities? Some of these may be the 'flip side' of your positive qualities, but which sometimes get out of control. A word of caution at this point: do not list specific skills that you do not have unless you feel that the lack of these skills is holding you back in a particular area.

List these assets and liabilities at random as they pop into your mind or as they are suggested to you by others. Do not attempt to organise them in any type of pattern other than under the major heading of asset or liability. At this point you are only 'brainstorming'.

ASSETS	LIABILITIES
Write down your assets in this column	Write down your liabilities in this column

Next go over both lists. Tick all of the items which relate to performance: the skills that you either have or do not have.

Now it is possible to make four separate lists: performance assets and performance liabilities, behaviour assets and behaviour liabilities.

Before you accept these lists as being accurate, ask your partner to go over them with you. It may be that some of the liabilities you listed have actually been overcome in the last few years.

PERFORMANCE	BEHAVIOUR
List all of your assets from the above column which involve performance	List your assets from the above column which involve behaviour

PERFORMANCE	BEHAVIOUR
List all of your liabilities from the above column which involve performance	List your liabilities from the above column which involve behaviour

As Christians we recognise that there is a great deal of hope in the behaviour category, because if our behaviour is less than God demands, we know that he will give the strength to change it to meet his demands.

If God could say to Paul 'my power is made perfect in weakness' (2 Corinthians 12:9), the same holds true for you. Naturally God is displeased with the sin in our life, but he has the power to translate even sinful experiences into something that will bring glory to him.

Do not take offence if your fiancée suggests you have a fault. Remember Proverbs 27:6, which says, 'The kisses of an enemy may be profuse, but faithful are the wounds of a friend.'

There is an old, familiar prayer which is appropriate here:

God grant me the serenity
to accept the things I cannot change,
the courage to change the things I can,
And the wisdom to know the difference.

Never lose sight of the fact that God himself selected the collection of assets and attributes which you now possess. You may feel that the collection is very incomplete and second-rate. However, he planned you as a unique person for a unique purpose.

Some things like our looks cannot easily be changed, but our appearance can be greatly improved simply through giving attention to good grooming and intelligently selecting our clothes.

Women have an even broader latitude for enhancing their appearance. A few pounds spent with a fashion and colour consultant is a good investment. Far too many people with a low self-image are poor stewards of their appearance. They seem to think everyone should look past their appearance and get to know the 'real person'. This places too much burden on others. It is almost as though one has to pass a test to be their friend. We do not have the right to test others.

Some Practical Steps

1 I feel rejected when you ....

....

....

....

2 I feel a sense of acceptance and worth when you... ....

....

. . . .

. . . .

3 Are you relying on your partner to meet needs that can only realistically be met by God?

. . . .

. . . .

4 Do you feel your partner is relying on you to meet needs that can only realistically be met by God?

. . . .

. . . .

Are there any further statements that you can add to your objectives on page 41?

Further reading

Dave and Joyce Ames, *Second Honeymoon* (Kingsway), Chapter 3.
Lawrence Crabb, *The Marriage Builder* (NavPress), Chapter 2.

MATURITY IS:

Applying the same standards to myself as I do to others.

Proverbs 20:23: 'The Lord detests differing weights, and dishonest scales do not please him.'

9

A Biblical Philosophy of Finances

Two questions must be answered before we can logically determine how we are going to handle any of our assets.

1 What do we expect from life?

2 How will we invest our life?

We cannot remember anyone ever asking us these questions and we are not sure we could have given a reasonable answer until we had been married nearly twenty years. As a result, there was a lot of wastage in every area of our lives. Finance was no exception. However, the very fact that you are reading this proves that you are doing a lot more to prepare for life, and marriage in particular, from a Christian perspective. You will be light years ahead.

We would now answer question 1, 'To develop the character of Christ', and 2, 'In the Great Commission' (making disciples, helping others to maturity in Christ). This is our basis for the following.

1 The first step to developing a Christian philosophy of finance would be to commit ourselves to developing the character of Christ in our own lives and helping others do the same.

2 The next step would be to transfer the ownership of all our assets to God. This includes our time, money, possessions and earning power.

One logical reason for this, besides the fact that we naturally want to relate our assets to our goals, is because God takes good care of his property. This means that if we transfer it all to him in complete genuineness, he is then responsible for it.

3 Establish God's word as the final authority in all financial matters. There are some great differences between a secular and a Christian world-view regarding finances. As with any other area of living, we need

to commit ourselves to a Christian world-view and not be tempted to borrow from secular philosophy.

4 Establish the tithe as a constant reminder that everything belongs to him. Malachi 3:10 and 11 says ' "Bring the whole tithe into the storehouse, that there may be food in my house. Test me in this," says the Lord Almighty, "and see if I will not throw open the floodgates of heaven and pour out so much blessing that you will not have room enough for it. I will prevent pests from devouring your crops, and the vines in your fields will not cast their fruit," says the Lord Almighty.'

It is reasonable to assume that the storehouse is our local church. In unique circumstances, where some might disagree, they may feel led to support a Christian organisation. Regardless of whether it is a tithe or an offering over and above, it is good to analyse the sorts of places where we ought to be giving God's money. That is what stewardship is all about.

First, do their goals take the Great Commission seriously? Are they actually helping people to maturity in Christ?

Are they relating all their assets to their goals? It is one thing to say we have a goal; it is another to actually act on it.

Is the leadership reflecting the character of Christ in their lives?

Are people responding positively to the message? If these things are true, the character of Christ is being reproduced and the organisation will be reproducing itself.

And last, is there a standard of excellence and a freedom from waste?

We must also remember that the Bible has more to say about giving to meet the needs of other individuals than it does about supporting Christian institutions. Since all we have belongs to God, we must be open to respond to the needs of others. We are not advocates of the 'prosperity gospel', but we do recognise that the people God definitely seems to entrust with finances are those whom he can trust to hold them with an open hand.

5 Establish an atmosphere of mutual ownership. We generally promise each other all our worldly goods. This is the financial expression of oneness. Unfortunately many couples make that pledge and then proceed to deal with their finances in a very 'his and hers' mode. There is a lot of justification for his and hers clothes and various other personal items, but we always feel that couples who continue to deal with their finances in this way are missing a part of the oneness that others experience.

Also, there is the situation where a wife may not feel she can really give her husband a present because the funds she would be spending would actually be his. They may have a joint account but she feels that it is his money because he earned it. Think about it: if marriage is a partnership, the fact that one may be functioning in a responsibility that provides the income does not entitle that partner to sole ownership. Nor should the other partner feel they are the object of the charity of some 'big benevolent bread winner'. The wife is no less entitled to share in the family income just because she has assumed responsibilities in the 'non-profit' segment. She earns her keep and more.

It is not the amount of money we earn which determines our financial stability, but the way we spend it. We have marvelled over the years at the couples who, with very humble means, managed modest but lovely homes and were never financially embarrassed. Yet others with five times the income were always short of funds.

6 Evaluate expenditures in terms of achieving our goals. We need to develop a long-range focus on the way we spend our money. Will this purchase help us towards our goal? We must learn to separate our *needs* from our *wants*. For instance, we may need to upgrade our car because of a lot of travelling involved in our occupation or ministry, but does that justify the de luxe model? That is just a want.

7 Develop sales resistance. Advertising is certainly a legitimate business, but there is a sense in which its goal is to raise the lust factor to a level where we feel we need something today that we did not know existed yesterday. Many couples find a good way to avoid impulsive spending is to agree on a limit of, say £5 or £10 as all that can be spent without consulting the other partner.

We have to remember that every time we make a purchase, we are converting our assets, which are very compact, and have the ability to maintain us through the interest they accrue, into bulky or fragile items which require maintenance, space and insurance.

There are times when we need to ask ourselves if our use would actually justify a purchase, or might it be better to rent it? Many recreation items such as caravans and boats that are on hire purchase are used so seldom they could be rented over the course of the hire purchase scheme and with enough cash left over to buy the item new if we still wanted one. In the meantime we would have saved insurance, maintenance and depreciation costs.

Other questions we need to ask are:

Does the product do what it claims it will do?

Are we buying more than we need?

Is there a better way to buy it?

'I was once £400 lying in your bank account collecting interest—see how I've grown. Now I occupy space in your lounge collecting dust. Now that I'm a family member I'll expect to be properly insured and have a maintenance contract.'

Is there some way to receive counsel about this purchase? For example, if you are not mechanically inclined it makes sense to obtain the counsel of someone who is before buying a car.

8 Do not be afraid of home maintenance jobs. Some household maintenance jobs may be beyond a young husband's understanding but again this is an area where wise counsel can be recruited from the local body of Christ.

9 Make it one of your financial goals to stay out of debt altogether and never borrow money for depreciating items. Cars seem to be the most difficult thing to purchase on a cash basis. However, by carefully working our way up in the quality of cars we drive we can usually afford to wait until we can pay cash in the price range that suits us. Then if we

begin to make car payments to ourselves, we can replace that car when necessary. We find that the bank is actually paying interest to us rather than us paying interest to the bank. It may sound impossible but it is not.

Few people would ever own a home if they could not have a mortgage. In fact house prices have reached such proportions in some areas that many engaged couples have had to postpone their weddings. But for the most part a house is not a depreciating item. With wise counsel a couple can buy a home that will be appreciating in value so that if it was ever necessary to sell in a hurry they would still not lose money.

There are several scriptures involved, such as Romans 13:8 which tells us, 'Let no debt remain outstanding, except the continuing debt to love one another.' And Proverbs 22:7 says, 'The borrower is slave to the lender.' However, there is an even stronger reason given in James 4:13 and 14: 'Now listen, you who say, "Today or tomorrow we will go to this or that city, spend a year there, carry on business and make money." Why, you do not even know what will happen tomorrow. What is your life? You are a mist that appears for a little while and then vanishes.'

This talks about presuming on the future. Financially, presuming on the future can cause us to lose our flexibility to serve God at any place and in any way he may require of us.

It is easy, with the credit now being offered, to get a house full of new furniture and a washing machine on HP, but this can lead to financial bondage. A couple who watch the classified ads can make some outstanding furniture buys. A house that is furnished with good quality used furniture is generally much more interesting and more tastefully decorated than when twice the money is spent on new furniture that may not be a tenth of the quality. Even period furniture is available through this means—we furnished our first few places in 'early poverty'.

When we were first married we did not have a budget; we thought that was only for those with money. We lived very hand to mouth. We finally realised that even on our meagre sum we could avoid having too much month left over at the end of our money. Even then we would play it a bit too close and find that some unforeseen emergency would send us scrambling around looking for something we could sell to avoid starvation.

We finally realised that we could avoid even that embarrassment by giving ourselves breathing space. We do not dare budget every penny of our income. In fact, it is best if we actually have three separate accounts. That may sound a bit over the top, but do not tune out yet.

A current account to pay the bills as they arrive,

A back-up account with sufficient funds to cover the inevitable emergency—the car will need repairs, water heaters have to be replaced, washing machines require repair etc. Therefore we need to have £300 to £500 put back to cover these eventualities. This may sound impossible, but if there is a distinct possibility that this will eventually be needed, why not make it a goal to begin establishing such a fund now? **An investment account**, which is entirely separate from the rest, is where we save for that better car, or holiday, or for a down payment on a house. You may not feel this will apply to you for some time. It did not with us for years and years, but then not everyone will take as long to get their act together financially.

The lack of funds causes poverty. Financial bondage is caused by a lack of contentment and poor stewardship.

Remember: **it is not the amount of money we earn which determines our financial stability, but the way we spend it.**

Some Practical Steps

1 How will we go about deciding which are needs and which are wants?

....

....

....

....

2 Am I committed to consistent communication about the way we handle our finances, giving, earning, spending and saving?

....

3 Would you be more comfortable if your partner maintained the cheque-book, or would you rather do it? Explain.

....

....

4 Do you see any justification for any type of separate accounts or funds?

....

....

....

5 Is the concept of a current account to pay bills, a back-up account for emergencies and a long-range savings account something we want to adopt?

. . . .

. . . .

6 What do you consider a tithe? Are you committed to tithing? What about additional offerings?

. . . .

. . . .

. . . .

7 What would you consider justifiable reasons for going into debt?

. . . .

. . . .

. . . .

I would be most likely to be extravagant on the following:	I would be more likely to attempt to skimp on the following:
____ A house	____ A house
____ Furniture	____ Furniture
____ A car	____ A car
____ Clothes	____ Clothes
____ Jewellery and accessories	____ Jewellery and accessories
____ Sports/hobby	____ Sports/hobby
____ Appliances	____ Appliances
____ Tools	____ Tools
____ Books	____ Books
____ Holidays	____ Holidays
____ Food	____ Food

Add other items to either list as necessary.

Are there any further statements that you can add to your objectives on page 41?

Further reading

Dave and Joyce Ames, *Second Honeymoon* (Kingsway), Chapter 10.
Joyce Huggett, *Two Into One* (IVP), Chapter 13.

MATURITY IS:

Retaining my financial freedom by purposing not to jeopardise future earnings through credit spending.

Proverbs 22:7: 'The rich rule over the poor, and the borrower is servant to the lender.'

10

Giving and Receiving Forgiveness

Frequently couples at their golden wedding celebration will say something to the effect of 'we made it a point never to go to bed angry'. This paraphrase of Paul's words in Ephesians 4:26 guaranteed they not only resolved conflicts but also gave and received forgiveness. Forgiveness is one of the most central and yet one of the least understood of all Christian teachings.

It begins by understanding a basic biblical concept: **life is not ruined by the sins committed against us but by the way we respond to those sins.**

When we are sinned against we have a decision either to forgive or harbour resentment. If we choose the latter the natural result is bitterness. Bitterness not only results from our response to an offence; it can also result from the notion that life has not treated us fairly. 'Our plans have fallen through.' 'Nothing seems to go right and everyone else is better off than we are.' 'Let's face it, we have been unjustly penalised in the game of life.' It gets progressively worse until we are genuinely bitter. Some never recognise that they are actually angry with God. They will not forgive him.

There are four fairly essential bits of information to consider when we are faced with a decision requiring forgiveness:

1 God is sovereign.
2 Forgiveness is non-optional.
3 Bitterness is costly.
4 Forgiveness is a decision.

1 God is sovereign. This means that he is always in control: he never takes a holiday from his responsibilities. It also means he has a plan and the power to see that his plan is implemented. Isaiah 14:27 says 'For the

Lord Almighty has purposed, and who can thwart him? His hand is stretched out, and who can turn it back?'

Most of us are aware of verses that speak of the sovereignty of God. Many of us can quote Romans 8:28: 'In all things God works for the good of those who love him, who have been called according to his purpose.' But it helps even more if we understand what his purpose is, which is in the next verse: 'Those God foreknew he also predestined to be conformed to the likeness of his Son, that he might be the firstborn among many brothers.'

God's goal for every Christian is that we develop the character of Christ. Consequently God is more committed to our character than he is to our comfort. Knowing his plan is to develop the character of Christ in my life, I can much more easily say 'What are you trying to teach me Lord?' when I am offended, instead of my natural 'Why me Lord?'

'What are you trying to teach me Lord?' recognises the sovereignty of God. 'Why me Lord?' is asking God if he was out to lunch when this painful incident occurred.

Understanding that God is sovereign, one may question, where was God when a child was molested? Where was God when a woman was raped? Where was God when there was an unnecessary killing? The answer is, God was there. Why he allows those things we just do not know. But we do know God is present, if we have accepted his word as the final authority on his character. When trials come we must trust what he has revealed about himself in the Bible rather than what our senses tell us at that particular point in time.

In April 1986 our 29-year-old son met a lorry coming from the opposite direction with a very heavy utility trailer in tow. The driver had forgotten to fasten the safety chain and the trailer came loose, bounced against the side of a bridge and then ricocheted across to our son's lane, killing him instantly.

On our journey to the funeral we all did a lot of thinking. Our daughter wanted me (Dave) to preach at the funeral because she said, 'I don't want my brother's death to have been a total loss. I want his mates to hear the gospel and besides that Billy would not want a sad funeral, so I think you should preach, Dad.' I had to come to grips with a lot of things in a hurry. I had to come to grips with how my understanding of the sovereignty of God applied in that situation. Was God out to lunch when this happened?

If I could not believe in the sovereignty of God when it was my son lying there how could I tell someone who came for counselling, suffering the whims of a very insensitive partner, 'You continue to honour God in this situation. Continue to love. God is sovereign. He's keeping score.

He knows what's happening in your life and your marriage.' How could I say that if I did not really believe God was sovereign when something affected me? In other words, I have to hang on to what God says about himself. I have no other authority.

We found out later on there was some benefit from this. Not the kind of benefit that we would have traded our son for, but no longer can anyone look at us when we try to console their loss of a child and say, 'But you don't understand'. Because we do. We paid the price to join a very exclusive society. We did not want to join it because the dues were too high. But God wanted us in that society and we now have a choice. We can either accept that God is sovereign and recognise that this is part of his plan, or we can have a pity party and completely neutralise everything God wants to do through us.

We have some friends whose 21-year-old daughter was murdered by a boyfriend who threw her out of a third-storey window. They had a lot to come to grips with. This was a Christian couple who have a testimony, but they were suddenly faced with a choice. They could forgive this young man, just as we had to forgive the man who failed to secure his trailer, or they could allow bitterness to completely neutralise everything God was doing in their lives. They recognised that God is sovereign and that they had to forgive, and they did.

Our personal choice for the most effective sermon of this decade goes to Gordon Wilson of Enniskillen. On prime time news coverage he very convincingly forgave the IRA bomber who killed his daughter. The world is looking for evidence that Christianity makes a difference.

2 Forgiveness is non-optional Matthew 6:14 says, 'If you forgive men when they sin against you, your heavenly Father will also forgive you. But *if you do not forgive men their sins, your heavenly Father will not forgive your sins.'* We pray quite frequently, 'Forgive us our sins as we forgive those who sin against us.' It is a proportional thing. I would not pray that prayer if I was going to continue to hold something against someone. It would be very dangerous, which is the next point.

3 Bitterness is costly—because it costs us our fellowship with God. We cannot say, 'You and I are all right Lord. It's just my partner I can't live with.' This immediately cuts us off from God. When our unforgiveness cuts us off from our brother we are automatically cut off from God. Spiritually it costs us our fellowship.

Psychologically it is costly because we are in bondage to the person we will not forgive.

'Who says bitterness is costly. I'm only 38, but because people think I'm an OAP I get reduced rates.'

Physically it is costly because it has been proven to cause ulcers, arthritis and all sorts of other conditions. Dr S I MacMillan, in his book *None of These Diseases*, makes it plain that bitterness releases certain hormones that can cause disease, including arthritis, in almost any organ in the body.[1] Any of the above is a high price to pay to exercise our right to unforgiveness.

4 Forgiveness is a decision. It is a decision to make a commitment not to bring the offence up against the individual any longer, a commitment not to hold it against the person, to separate the sin from the sinner.

Often we confuse forgiving and forgetting. We get this idea because God says, 'I will remember their sins no more.' Let us analyse this. Does the God who knows everything about anything not know something that I know? God forgave my sins yesterday and I still remember them; does he have amnesia? Obviously this is a Jewish hyperbole. What does it mean?

In big corporations it is not possible just to fire someone. There must be a lot of documentation. Problematic employees are given letters of counselling which are filed in an unfavourable information folder. Then if enough information is amassed they can be sacked without the union going on strike.

When God forgives us he tears up our unfavourable information folder. He remembers it, but he does not have it on file against us any

[1] S I MacMillan, *None of These Diseases* (Marshall, Morgan & Scott: Basingstoke, 1963), p 73.

longer. When we need to forgive someone else we know we cannot just forget it right away, but we can certainly say it is not on file against them any more. We can tear up the unfavourable information folder. We hate doing this because it could be handy information in the event the other party ever accuses us of a transgression.

When we find this extremely difficult, there are a few things we can do to make it easier.

First, we can make a list of the things that we are holding against others, things that are bothering us, causing pain, things that make life miserable. Then analyse each one of them for a lesson. 'What were you trying to teach me in this Lord?' Because God is sovereign, this other person may well have been a tool in God's hand to try to get our attention about a particular problem we are having. In other words, the offence may have been, to some degree, justified.

Then list the problem areas that God is dealing with in our life. This should help to put the offences from the first list in perspective. People who have difficulty forgiving are usually people who fail to recognise their own sin.

Then, by an act of the will, forgive this other person or persons. Tear up both lists. Make a commitment never to bring this up against them again. Try to remember this person without remembering the act. It is not going to happen all at once, so we have to hark back to that original commitment and say, 'I've made a commitment not to bring this up any more, not to hold it against them.'

Then find a way to demonstrate your new attitude. Find a way to let this person (who could be your partner) know that you love them and that you have forgiven them. You may not be able to actually tell them. For example, 'I forgive you for being so patronising towards me' would make them feel that they were having their sins confessed to them.

Some Practical Considerations

During courtship couples frequently view each other with an exaggerated positive focus. When reality actually arrives (and it always does) the contrast between it and the exaggerated positive focus is sometimes so great as to produce a distorted negative focus. This disillusion causes one to feel neglected, slighted, rejected, etc. Chances are things are not as bad as they appear—it is only the contrast. It is time to take a realistic assessment of your partner. So he/she does have some faults—they still have the positive qualities you saw before. The main thing is not to allow resentment to build up in your thought life to eat away at your relationship. This is why it is so important to address each day those things that are bugging us. Resentment will colour our attitude towards our partner and will show itself in a lack of respect and lack of desire to make love. It is very difficult to make love with someone you resent.

Some Practical Steps

1 Do you believe that this could possibly happen in your marriage?

....

2 What will you do to prevent it happening?

....

....

....

3 Are there issues in your relationship at the present time that you resent? Are you willing to forgive and put them behind you?

....

....

....

Is there any other relationship that is marred by unforgiveness? It would be best for you and your intended to pray through this to avoid any residual bitterness entering your marriage. See Hebrews 12:15.

A Clear Conscience

A close companion to a forgiving spirit is a clear conscience. Both are necessary in a relationship because bitterness and guilt are equally impenetrable barriers used by the Enemy to separate husband and wife, even when the offence is not against a partner.

A clear conscience is a transparency resulting from the knowledge that all past wrongs have been put right.

When this transparency is destroyed we are unable to practise the vulnerability necessary to maintain an intimate relationship. The fact that one has a clear conscience is not always a sign of right responses to the trials and temptations of life so much as an appropriate response to sin and guilt. 1 John 1:9 tells us, 'If we confess our sins, he is faithful and just and will forgive us our sins and purify us from all unrighteousness.'

Frequently we find God requiring more of us than confessing the sin to him. Matthew 5:23 and 24 tells us, 'Therefore, if you are offering your gift at the altar and there remember that your brother has something against you, leave the gift there in front of the altar. First go and be reconciled to your brother; then come and offer your gift.' It is as if the Lord were saying 'you have told me how wrong you were, now go and tell your partner.'

This text makes us aware that God is more interested in relationships than in religious worship: 'first go and be reconciled.' Couple this with Matthew 18:15 on confrontation: 'If your brother sins against you, go and show him his fault....' We can see that God wants us to take the initiative to put things right no matter who is at fault.

A guilty conscience is apparent to its owner. Failure to clear it can only add to the guilt because it is also robbing a relationship the transparency that it lives on. Therefore two suffer for the guilt of one.

The main consideration in gaining a clear conscience is that we work out the wording carefully in advance as the prodigal son did when he was off in the far country. Things such as 'If I have been wrong, please forgive me' or attempts to share the blame with others are ineffective in restoring trust. The following three-part concept has helped thousands to put things right.

I was wrong (in the way I spoke to you last night).
It was (insensitive).
Will you please forgive me?

This assumes full responsibility, identifies the offence, both specifically (the way I spoke) and the basic offence (insensitivity) and it requests forgiveness.

'I was wrong' are the three hardest words in English to put together, but they raise no barriers. Identifying the sin or offence lets the other person know you understand something of the hurt. The question mark at the end requires a response, helping the offended party to fulfil their scriptural obligation to forgive.

A word of caution: we dare not simply burst in on others with a glibly phrased formula and expect them to be warm with forgiveness. Our action must reflect an attitude of genuine sorrow for causing them pain or inconvenience.

Some More Practical Steps

4 Is there anything which your intended should know that you have not revealed to this point?

....

....

....

5 Is there anything which needs to be cleared up with someone else that is robbing you of a clear conscience? It might be helpful for you to pray together as a couple for God's direction. (Note this may not be anything to do with this relationship but it can affect it.)

....

....

....

Are there any further statements that you can add to your objectives on page 41?

Further reading

Dave and Joyce Ames, *Second Honeymoon* (Kingsway), Chapters 11 and 12.
Ed Wheat, *Love Life for Every Married Couple* (Marshalls), Chapter 14.
Joyce Huggett, *Marriage on the Mend* (Kingsway), Chapter 8.
Joyce Huggett, *Conflict, Friend or Foe* (Kingsway), Chapters 5 and 12.

MATURITY IS:

Resisting the temptation to 'get even'.

Proverbs 20:22: 'Do not say, "I'll pay you back for this wrong!" Wait for the Lord, and he will deliver you.'

11

Sexual Love

It is obvious that one chapter in a workbook cannot be very comprehensive on any one subject and we certainly hope that you will be involved in some further reading from the suggested reading list. However, it is possible to come to grips with the key factors to facilitate meaningful negotiation.

The two most important factors about sexual relations are: **Fulfilling sexual relations are the result of giving rather than getting. Men and women are different.** This second statement would seem obvious, but many trip over the obvious, so we will be looking at some of the differences.

The first is the Christian position which is 180 degrees out of phase with the world. It makes us much more sensitive to the second, which is a biological, psychological observation available to every pagan.

1 Corinthians 7:3–5 is the key passage on this. 'The husband should fulfil his marital duty to his wife, and likewise the wife to her husband. The wife's body does not belong to her alone but also to her husband. In the same way, the husband's body does not belong to him alone but also to his wife. Do not deprive each other except by mutual consent for a time, so that you may devote yourselves to prayer. Then come together again so that Satan will not tempt you because of your lack of self-control.'

This passage shifts our focus from human rights to human responsibilities. The spirit of the age is, 'I have needs and I have a right to have my needs met'. The Christian focus is, 'I have a responsibility to meet my partner's needs'. This subtlety, this difference, is extremely profound and far-reaching. It brings us all the way back to the basic concept of human selfishness and the selflessness which typifies the agape love which God demands as well as empowers.

Strangely enough, it is the selfless focus on sex which continues to provide the ultimate satisfaction in a pure and simple way even after thirty, forty and fifty years of marriage, while the self-centred focus not only fails to produce what it promises but often leaves the participants in bondage.

If you have a somewhat limited understanding of sex you may have wondered why people contrive to incorporate such things as whips, chains, handcuffs and strange costumes into their sexual relations. The answer is, the desire to please oneself is always expanded rather than fulfilled, which means it quickly loses appreciation of the normal and seeks the exotic.

Conversely, the focus to please one's partner brings personal pleasure proportionate with achieving the goal. In other words, if my goal is to please my partner, the more pleasure my partner receives, the more this adds to my pleasure. It is the distinction of focus between self and partner which is the difference between making love, and people using each other's bodies in mutual masturbation.

The concept of casual recreational sex in society sends young people out into the streets and into bars endeavouring to establish relationships which lead to the bedroom. The Christian concept reverses this: we see sexual intercourse as the celebration of a relationship rather than the purpose of it.

The world has distorted this, and unfortunately many Christians have responded in a very reactionary manner causing many to throw the baby out with the bath water. In many instances the church has projected the attitude that although God invented sex he does not really approve of it. Or that the only purpose of it is for procreation, which is obviously disproved in the above passage.

Love is meeting needs, which means that anyone motivated to love automatically assumes a burden to discover what the needs are. The fact that our partner is of the opposite sex automatically means we must familiarise ourselves with the *general* information on the basic differences. However, the fact that our partner is another unique human being means that our partner also has unique and specific needs not necessarily covered in the broad-brush approach of male and female.

One main gender distinction seems to be that sexual relations with women are much more psychological than biological, whereas with men the reverse seems to be true. This explains why women place a high priority on the right words, soft music, anything that can generally be attributed to romance. It explains why women can be aroused by running a finger over their shoulders but men fail to appreciate anything not concentrated on their genital area.

This lays the groundwork for another great factor that is frequently ignored at great expense: because women must have these psychological or romantic preconditions met before they can enter fully into sexual relations, they take a lot longer to 'warm up'.

A woman who feels ignored all evening because her husband is preoccupied with his own thoughts or interests is not going to be interested in love-making when she goes to bed. Some time needs to be spent in conversation so that she feels he desires the total person and not just the body.

It is only through learning and understanding these considerations that we can really love our partner sexually. Frequently husbands and wives will attempt to arouse each other in a way that would suit them personally and this causes problems. For instance, a woman may not understand why her husband's only response is frustration when she rubs her fingers over his shoulder. Conversely, she may recoil completely if he seems oblivious to every other need that she has and reaches straight for her genital area. Both consider the other to be highly insensitive.

Sexual relations are the physical and emotional expression of the intellectual concept that competitiveness has no place in marriage. Sexual relations have been called 'a non-competitive contact body sport', which is simply a light-hearted way of emphasising the fact that competition is not involved. In fact, one of the reasons God is so concerned that we do not involve ourselves in premarital and extramarital relations is so that we will never feel we are competing against the skill and ability of another lover.

This allows us to enter into this exercise in vulnerability which amounts to helping each other take off our emotional armour. Because it is the celebration of a relationship, this physical vulnerability functions best on a foundation of psychological and spiritual vulnerability. In other words, the fact that we can be open, honest and sharing with each other intellectually, emotionally and spiritually means that we have a sound basis for open, vulnerable sharing physically.

This vulnerable state requires that we have a climate of service in our relationship, that we are committed to serving one another. Servanthood has been defined as being excited about making someone else successful. As such it is the physical outworking of our commitment to love.

'Sexual love involves taking off the emotional armour.'

There must also be a certain transparent suspense about our sexual relations. The fact that we give each other little clues, invitations and propositions, gives a transparency to our motives, but it also builds excitement and suspense about the actual unveiling of each coming together.

There must also be a colour of adventure about sexual relations. Although we certainly want to give each other a basis for anticipation, nothing could be more boring than having sex scheduled for every Tuesday night. Nothing could be more deadly than to be able to anticipate every move our partner will make. Reading through the Song of Solomon we find the Hebrew concept of sex one of great adventure and delight. We should strive for the same sense of adventure.

For instance, there is nothing in the Bible that requires us to make love in the bedroom. It is of the utmost importance that we continually experiment with things such as venue, lighting, perfumes etc. Not only is it not necessary to confine sex to the bedroom, it is disastrous to associate sexual activity with 'going to bed'. Foreplay, that which stimulates our partner towards sexual intercourse, should begin long before bedtime, possibly at breakfast. One of the most common mistakes is beginning foreplay after the lights go out for the night.

Communicating on sex can be difficult. Many find it very embarrassing to describe their expectations regarding actual physical technique. Those who find verbal communication difficult will have to rely on what we call corporal communication.

The best illustration for this was our cat Sam. Sam had a one-word vocabulary and yet he found no problem with making it perfectly clear whether he would prefer to be scratched under his chin, behind the ears, or on his tummy. He just simply moved his body in ways that communicated more effectively than words.

Then if we go on a step further and consider that Paul says the wife's body does not belong to her alone, that means the husband must have some authority to move the limbs around in various patterns. Naturally the wife has the responsibility to make such comments as, 'The leg won't bend that way.'

One major consideration with this type of communication is that when we disagree with something that is being communicated, we do not abruptly pull away or jump. Just say softly, 'I'm not ready for that yet. Wait a few minutes,' or 'Wait three years,' whatever is appropriate. How to express approval can be left to the imagination.

There are a few common barriers to the satisfying sex life. Physically the state of our health and the amount of energy are very limiting factors. At the early end of parenting women can spend literally years in a state of near exhaustion, which for them can make sexual relations very unattractive. Husbands need to be understanding of this and both need to work out some sort of plan or schedule of rest for her. If the wife is unable to take a nap in the afternoon when the children are napping, then possibly there is someone who could look after them for a few hours at least one day a week for her to regain her strength.

Men are not quite so easily put off sex. The fact that they may be running a fever or worn out is frequently an insufficient deterrent, which may mean he can lose patience with the wife's reluctance.

Another physical barrier to good sex is poor hygiene. This is undoubtedly the most intimate physical contact two human beings can have and it requires sweet breath, which means freshly brushed teeth. It also means having a wash just before entering into such activity. It is a part of loving consideration. Men who work with their hands might find a little attention with hand lotion could make them much more romantically stimulating.

Intellectually, we may be the victims of wrong thinking. We may be suffering from the concept that sex was invented by the publishers of *Playboy* magazine rather than God, and this needs to be dealt with.

Spiritually, we may be out of fellowship with God and therefore find fellowship with our partner difficult. We have found it amazing over the years how our spiritual relationship affects our physical relationship.

Emotionally, a partner may have been molested or abused, meaning that sexual contact sends mixed signals, developing inappropriate emotions. This is no small problem and the emotional blockage is very real, but is certainly something we do not have to live with. There is no reason that any child of God should be a victim of their past. We have seen a lot of prayers answered in this area.

One of the first things that should be done is to share this with your partner so that your partner can help separate fact from fiction and be sensitive. The next thing is to make sure that the sin committed against you is not causing you in turn to sin. In other words, it would be good to review the forgiveness chapter and apply it towards that person who created the original problem.

Also, emotionally it is very important that we do not carry resentment towards each other. It is very easy to allow minor offences to become bricks in a wall between the two of us. This is why it is so important that we practise confrontation. The more we use phrases such as 'I have a problem I think you can help me with', the fewer problems we will have in the bedroom.

One last consideration—many couples have experienced total loss of desire and even a repugnance towards sex with no apparent reason. This frequently turns out to be a manifestation of the fact that Satanists are praying for the breakdown of Christian marriage. This has happened to us and has been reported to us by many other couples. The solution is first of all complete honesty. This lack of interest may only be on the part of one partner. If you feel this way do not let it go very long without confessing it. The action, as with any spiritual warfare situation, is to pray together taking authority over the Enemy in this particular area.

There are many areas of sexual activity where the Bible is silent; it neither condones or condemns them. It is the spirit of the 1 Corinthians 7 passage which helps us unravel the appropriateness of such things as oral sex, anal sex, and masturbation. Does this meet my partner's needs or only serve my own? Masturbation, for instance, does nothing for our partner and tends to make us independent of our partner.

Some Practical Steps

1 Study 1 Corinthians 7:2–5 and 9 considering the following questions:
What seems to be the purpose of sexual relations in this passage?

. . . .

. . . .

Does the Bible consider sexual desire to be normal? . . . .
What is God's answer to it?

. . . .

. . . .

Is having these desires satisfied a 'marriage right'?

. . . .

Would 'marriage responsibilities' be a better term and if so why?

. . . .

. . . .

This passage identifies the basic concept which makes the difference between the secular philosophy of sex in marriage and the Christian outlook. What is it?

. . . .

. . . .

Should couples discuss their desires and if so why?

. . . .

. . . .

How long should they abstain from sexual relations?

. . . .

. . . .

2 Is there a principle in Acts 20:35 that can be applied in marital sexual relationships?

. . . .

. . . .

3 Compare 1 Corinthians 7:2–5, Proverbs 5:15–19, Genesis 1:27, 28 and 2:23, 24. List three purposes for sex.

a . . . .

b . . . .

c . . . .

4 Study Philippians 2:3–4 and state specifically how this passage may be applied to marital (sexual) relations.

. . . .

. . . .

. . . .

5 Study the Song of Songs 1:2 and 13–16. Then study chapter 7. What does this tell us about a biblical attitude regarding our partner's body in the marriage relationship?

....

....

....

6 What attitudes towards the marriage partner and his/her body are suggested by the Song of Songs 4:1–7 and 5:10–16?

....

....

....

Should a marriage partner be embarrassed or ashamed because he/she finds delight in his/her partner? Is it proper to be excited about, to anticipate and enjoy sexual relations with one's spouse?

....

....

....

7 'We have sex every night. My husband won't take no even when I am unwell. I say sex, not love-making, for that is what it has become, just the same old act. I do love him and would value some helpful instruction.' Is this couple's problem simply different expectations regarding the frequency of sexual relations or does it go deeper? Explain your answer.

....

....

....

Contraception is a very controversial subject even among Christians. All sides seem to be confident of biblical grounds for their various positions. However, one area of agreement is that intra-uterine devices are unacceptable. The fact is that they hold the uterus open, which means that egg and sperm are allowed to unite, but the pregnancy is doomed because it cannot be sustained without the uterus closing. This means that these devices actually allow pregnancies to begin and then abort them, a notion out of line with biblical concepts.

It would seem that there is a lot of ground to explore in determining a suitable method of contraception.

8 Which method do you think you would feel the most comfortable using in your marriage? ....

9 Do you have any anxiety as you anticipate sexual relations?

....

....

....

Are there any further statements that you can add to your objectives on page 41?

Further reading

Dave and Joyce Ames, *Second Honeymoon* (Kingsway), Chapter 15.
Ed Wheat, *Love Life for Every Married Couple* (Marshalls), Chapter 6.
Tim and Beverly LaHaye, *The Act Of Marriage* (Zondervan), Chapters 2 and 3.
Joyce Huggett, *Two Into One* (IVP), Chapter 9.
Joyce Huggett, *Marriage on the Mend* (Kingsway), Chapter 7.
Joyce Huggett, *Conflict, Friend or Foe?* (Kingsway), Chapter 11.

MATURITY IS:

Recognising that no commandment of God was ever given to complicate life but to guarantee the quality of it.

Proverbs 6:32: 'But a man who commits adultery lacks judgment; whoever does so destroys himself.'

Notes

Marriage—The Early Years

by Ian & Ruth Coffey

Marriage means adjustment.

Emotionally—learning how to build a friendship together and adjust to another person's way of doing things.

Physically—discovering sexuality as a gift from God and learning how the best lovers give rather than take!

Socially—building a home together where others can find hospitality and friendship.

Spiritually—growing together in God and discovering your place in the local church.

It's all an exciting new challenge, and this book aims to equip you for your new life together.

IAN & RUTH COFFEY have been married for fifteen years, and have four sons. Ian is a Baptist minister and Field Director of the Evangelical Alliance; Ruth is a nurse and home-maker.

Kingsway Publications

Marriage As God Intended

by Selwyn Hughes

'We have never had an argument in the whole of our marriage,' said the husband.
'How did you accomplish that?' asked the counsellor.
'We just don't talk.'

Communication is only one of the problem areas faced by married couples—there can be many other difficulties that cause us to fall short of God's perfect plan.

This book offers help—not only with specific problems, but for improving what is already good and healthy.

There are chapters on:

- relationships with parents and in-laws
- who's the head of the family?
- sexual difficulties
- the temptation to adultery
- divorce and remarriage

Selwyn Hughes is highly respected as a leading marriage guidance counsellor. Here he draws on his many years' experience as both husband and counsellor, blending biblical principles with practical suggestions on how to let God keep your marriage at its best.

Kingsway Publications

Kingsway Publications

Kingsway Publications publishes books to encourage spiritual values in the home, church and society. The list includes Bibles, popular paperbacks, more specialist volumes, booklets, and a range of children's fiction.

Kingsway Publications is owned by The Servant Trust, a Christian charity run by representatives of the evangelical church in Britain, committed to serving God in publishing and music.

For further information on the Trust, including details of how you may be able to support its work, please write to:

The Secretary
The Servant Trust
1 St Anne's Road
Eastbourne
East Sussex BN21 3UN
England